IRON AGE:
THE ART OF GHOSTFACE KILLAH

DEAN VAN NGUYEN

Copyright © 2019 by Dean Van Nguyen

First published by
Headstuff,
5-6 Lombard Street East,
Dublin,
D02 WK73,
Ireland

All rights reserved. No part of this publication may be reproduced, distributed, or transmitted in any form or by any means, including photocopying, recording, or other electronic or mechanical methods, without the prior written permission of the publisher, except in the case of brief quotations embodied in critical reviews and certain other noncommercial uses permitted by copyright law.

ISBN: 978 1 09474 000 3

Copy editing by Kirsty Tobin

Cover artwork by John Breiner
Book design and typesetting by Aengus Tukel

Dedicated to all my family and friends, with us and departed, who've helped me along the way.

Thanks to Alan Bennett, Amy Bond, John Breiner, Elaine Burke, the District squad, Miles Marshall Lewis, David Ma, Kirsty Tobin, the Triumvirate, Aengus Tukel, Jeff Weiss, and Gabe Winogrond for their precious time, kind words, and positive energy on this project.

CONTENTS

Introduction: The Almighty	01
Line the Streets: The Genesis of Dennis Coles, New Yorker	05
Fast Life	22
Ghost Cinema	39
The Mask in the Iron Man	55
Comfortable Robes: On Ghostface Killah's Mighty Opus Fishscale	70
Life Changes: 8 Diagrams and the Fracturing of the Wu	77
Modern Beefs and the Capitalist Crush	87
Wake the Town and Tell the People	96
Afterword: A Letter From Staten Island	103
Bibliography	109

Introduction

THE ALMIGHTY

"Causin' terror, quick damage your whole era."

IN THE BEGINNING, HE WAS ONE OF NINE—THE WU-TANG clan's first swordsman, deployed on the first verse of the first song of the very first album. Ghostface Killah emerged with a mask bound to his face, skulking in the shadows as the Clan's concrete beats and doomed doctrine spread through the five boroughs and, later, across the entire planet. His fealty to the W was unquestioned, his blade a powerful weapon in the group's arsenal.

It was all there in that "Bring Da Ruckus" verse. *Enter the Wu-Tang (36 Chambers)* opened with one of its most poisonous darts. "Ghostface, catch the blast of a hype verse," the behemoth spits. "My Glock burst, leave in a hearse, I did worse." Ghost goes on to compare his toughness to an elephant's tusk, his trickiness to Nixon, and his explosiveness to the recent Waco, Texas, standoff between the ATF and David Koresh's Branch Davidian compound that ended in a huge fire, killing dozens. It was 1993 and you were listening to the sounds of the Wu-Tang Clan.

To a certain type of casual fan, Ghost remains just 11.11% of a greater entity. He shouldn't. The years slipped away and so did Ghost's mask. As members of the Clan revealed their individualism, he created the densest of solo catalogues. His career has often seen him butt heads with Clan allies while never abandoning his band of brothers. He is a rap legend within and outside the Wu. This book attempts to raise him further out of the pack and solidify his legacy.

But why is Dennis Coles the one? He did not write Wu scripture to the same extent that RZA did. Turn a camera on him and he doesn't possess the star quality of Method Man. If you were to ask what my highest-ranking album stamped with the Wu symbol is, it would be GZA's *Liquid Swords* all day. And when it comes to narrative punch, Raekwon is Ghost's equal. Yet whenever I'm asked who my favorite rapper of all time is, Ghost is the answer that just fits. I'd never say anyone spit as hard as Biggie, or was as captivating as MF DOOM. There are few artists who have made a better clutch of albums than Kanye West, or carried their star like Jay-Z, or sounded as earth-shatteringly righteous as Public Enemy. But if you unite all the key components that make up a rap artist—album-making, beat-picking, lyricism, story-telling, straight incredible rapping—one man stands alone.

Many components go into building one of the greatest rap artists of all time. This book will attempt to deconstruct the machine and examine Ghost's bionic make-up piece by piece.

Like his Wu-Tang brethren, Coles goes by many *noms de plume*: Tony Starks, Ironman, Pretty Toney, Ghostdini, Starky Love, the Wallabee Champ—the list goes on. But these monikers aren't arbitrary or skin deep. Each name gives an alternate glimpse of the man. He's like a photographer, constantly finding new angles from which to snap himself. Now, I'm trying to wrest control of the camera in an effort to capture all the elements that form

Ghost's indomitable artistry.

Call this an accompanying piece to his searing discography if you want to be really generous, but what follows is a series of essays that blend music criticism, cultural examination, and personal appreciation, focusing on one person out of nearly eight billion. It's the almighty Ghostface Killah. Who can deny him? Not a living soul.

LINE THE STREETS: THE GENESIS OF DENNIS COLES, NEW YORKER

"Pushing for the King of New York, I see it."

THE MOST MYTHOLOGIZED CITY ON THE PLANET IS DEFINED by 10,000 different images. A towering art deco structure. Travis Bickle's bright yellow chariot. The Ramones' tough leather sheathing. Youngblood Priest's 1971 customized Cadillac Eldorado. Each is a star in the constellation that is New York. There's no map that can chart the meaning of the city's every groove.

The Big Apple. Man, I can't have it. It's a piece of pamphlet language that pitches New York as a magical *terra firma* of Broadway lights, bright cocktails, and Sinatra fedoras. There's no such thing as the greatest city in the world. Beware anyone who tries to tell you that any geographical patch is the best of its kind—continent, country, whatever (*Late Show with David Letterman* gets a pass; those guys were allowed to call NYC the best). But New York must be the most lionized city in the world. A modern-day Tikal, but with better pizza slices.

The main thing I remember about my first trip was the heat. It was July 2007, and Manhattan's skyscrapers bore down like the walls of an oven. My friends and I ducked into retail stores to absorb the air conditioning before heading back out on our tourist voyage. The Statue of Liberty, Ellis Island—all that jazz. It was like striding onto a movie set. It seems possible to me that every inch of the city has, at some point, been captured on celluloid.

Every major city tries to structure itself as a series of tourist traps. Visitors face barriers they don't even know are there. They're siphoned into the centers with the best-funded museums, where upkeep is taken seriously and alcohol tends to be most expensive. New York is no different. There's a reason the most presentable buses service Times Square.

Before I set foot on US soil, the New York I knew seemed colder, more brutal. The East Coast hip-hop I copped as a kid gave me a fully fleshed-out, three-dimensional picture of the city. From Onyx's fiery vision of Jamaica, Queens, to The Notorious B.I.G.'s thrilling street narratives, to the Wu-Tang Clan's razor wire tales of Staten Island—each song was a vibrant polaroid of the city. A lot of the music was as cold as the subway cars that pulse through Gotham's arteries.

It was these icy streets that coaxed Dennis Coles into strapping a hockey mask onto his face. Legend has it that he used the eerie veil to avoid the authorities trying to hunt him down. Clan mythology is an undistillable mixture of truth and myth. All we can really be sure of is that the Staten Island native took the moniker Ghostface Killah and became one of the greatest rap artists to ever skulk the sidewalks of New York.

Ghost's music carried the DNA of his city while also helping to define it. His records are rarely described as 'New York albums' like, say, Nas's *Illmatic*, The Strokes' *Is This It?*, or the *Saturday Night Fever* soundtrack. Look up *The Village Voice's* "50 Most NYC

Albums Ever" and he's only there as part of the Clan on *Enter the Wu-Tang: 36 Chambers*. Yet Ghost's oeuvre both channels New York history and encapsulates it in the post-Clinton era. His music could only have been cultivated in this place and at this time.

The five boroughs spiritually connect as one, yet Staten Island is sometimes called the forgotten borough. It's a derisory nickname, ribbing on the region's relative anonymity when compared to Manhattan, Brooklyn, the Bronx or Queens. This makes sense geographically, though. Its residents are striking distance from the big city, but not so close that the skyscrapers loom over their roofs.

In 2008, State Senator Andrew J. Lanza announced plans to introduce legislation calling on Staten Island to secede from the rest of New York. The Republican—a representative of about two-thirds of the island at the time—said he was motivated to draft the bill because locals felt disproportionately burdened by high taxes and unimpressive city services. Residents had complained for years that they felt overlooked by the rest of the city, he claimed. Like an unloved stepchild sent to bed with no dinner.

"For Staten Islanders, it's undeniable that we get the short end of the stick, year after year, decade after decade," Lanza told *The New York Times*. "Being the smallest part of a large city, we always have to settle for crumbs. The focus is always on the other four boroughs. We have to fight twice as hard to get half as much."

Staten Island's history could almost be read as a microcosm of American sin. Italian Giovanni da Verrazzano was the first recorded European to lay eyes on the land in 1524, but the area remained mostly populated by Native Americans until about 1630, when the Dutch—calling the area Staaten Eylandt—attempted to establish settlements. There was the Pig War (1641), the Whiskey War (1642), and the Peach War (1655). Natives battled the European invaders trying to barge their way onto the land. From its origins, the region's history is soaked in blood.

In 1661, the Dutch established a lasting colony called Oude Dorp, or Old Town, near South Beach. The Dutch ceded the colony three years later as part of the treaty negotiations with England at the end of the Second Anglo-Dutch War. The English, as they do, officially anglicized Staaten Eylandt to Staten Island, and fused the land with their New York colony. Another three years later, the Native Americans also ceded any claims over Staten Island in an agreement with New York Governor Francis Lovelace. The English resurveyed much of the Dutch settlement to encourage the island's development, creating a new town named Nieuwe Dorp, now known as New Dorp. At the close of the 17th century, Staten Island's population was only 1,063.

On the shore of Upper New York Bay sits Stapleton, one of the older waterfront neighborhoods of the borough. On this land once stood the farm where one of the richest Americans in history, Cornelius Vanderbilt, grew up in the late 18th-early 19th century. You probably know already that the Vanderbilt name still carries significant heft.

Stapleton was built in the 1830s. Years before Ghostface Killah recorded a song called "Stapleton Sex," the area was Staten Island's commercial center and a popular place for southerners to visit. Some plantation owners would bring their cotton to New York to sell, or spend some time vacationing on the island with their families.

July 1863 saw six days of the Civil War Draft Riots. Spreading from Manhattan to Staten Island, Stapleton houses owned by black residents, who some viewed as responsible for the war, were torched. Black people were hunted down and beaten. According to SILive.com, five recorded deaths is a conservative estimate.

THE FORMAL NAME READS: THE NATION OF GODS AND earths. the more famous handle will always be the Five Percent

Nation. It was a movement small in scale but with a legacy that's proved everlasting.

Splintering off from the Nation of Islam in 1964, the Five Percenters culled some of its precursor's etiquette, recast the message of black empowerment, and put it all together in a streetwise package that to this day remains irresistible nectar for rap artists. The traditional elements of hip-hop are etched in stone: b-boying, emceeing, graffiti, DJing, and beatboxing. But sitting beneath the granite could have been a copy of Five Percent doctrine. That's the strength of the movement's ongoing influence on the culture.

In the 1990s, the Nation of Islam under Louis Farrakhan took steps to insert itself into hip-hop. Here's one story: In 1995, the organization's security wing—the Fruit of the Nation—stood guard as Eazy-E lay in Cedars-Sinai Medical Center dying of complications from AIDS. According to Ben Westhoff's book, *Original Gangstas*, even family members were denied access to the stricken West Coast legend.

In 2002, it was Farrakhan who delivered the keynote speech at the Hip-Hop Action Network's West Coast summit, an event organized to help address issues and needs facing the rap community. "All the children, they can't read *Dick and Jane*, but they can recite your raps," he said, as reported by *Billboard*. "They are three years old, and they start quoting you... suppose you started teaching children in your raps knowledge that the children need to know [in order] to fight in a racist society?" As recently as the release of Jay Z's fidelity-themed 4:44 in 2017, the 84-year-old Farrakhan was commenting on rap narratives.

Five decades before Jay teased the Nation of Islam's retired leader into making a public statement, Clarence 13X was unconvinced by the the organization. How could its mixed-race founder, Wallace Fard Muhammad, be God? Only a black man could fill that role and, in Clarence's mind, Fard did not qualify.

Let's go further back in time. The story of both the Nation of Islam and the Five Percenters begins in Detroit, 1930, when Fard seemingly springs up from Earth's rock fully formed. Nothing concrete is known about the man who, throughout the few years of his life that were recorded, went by about 50 different names. More mythos than mortal, Fard arrived out of thin air and disappeared into the sky. He was a figure you could build a holy faith around.

Fard's believed birthday, February 26th, is still known as Saviours' Day by the Nation. It's said Fard was born in 1877, making him at least 53-years-old in the small number of photographs that exist. The pictures might be old and grainy, but to me he looks far younger. Just another questionable strand in this ball of myth buttered in contradictions. A man pitched by a movement as God—not the embodiment of God or a messenger of God, but God himself.

At first, Fard moved around Detroit's poorest black neighborhoods, going door-to-door to sell silk. When invited into people's homes, he would lay out his new-age philosophy: Africa was their spiritual homeland and white Americans were the Devil who'd stolen their names and brainwashed them into worshipping a white-skinned savior. Fard soon advanced to preaching to crowds in basements. He gave his followers new names, telling them, as Michael Muhammad Knight writes in *Vice*, that they were "righteous Muslims by nature, the true heirs to the glories of a 'Nation of Islam' that was older than the sun, moon, and stars. They had no birth record, he told them. As black men, they were the fathers of civilization, gods of the universe."

Fard vanished off the face of the planet in 1934. Dropped off at the airport by his Supreme Minister, whom he had named Elijah Muhammad, Fard entrusted the student to continue his work before disappearing into the cosmos. According to the Nation of Islam's website, he instructed Muhammad to go to the Library of Congress in Washington, D.C. to research 104 books on the religion of Islam, among other subjects.

ORIGINALLY FROM VIRGINIA, 18-YEAR-OLD CLARENCE EDWARD Smith arrived in Harlem in 1946. He later enlisted in the Army, serving in the Korean War. By the time he returned to New York, the Nation of Islam under Elijah Muhammad had spread to the city. Smith, recast as Clarence 13X, became a key figure in the organization's Temple Number Seven in Harlem around the same time that Malcolm X was serving there as a minister, but split in 1963 over disagreements on the nature and identity of God.

Taking to the streets to preach his own interpretations of N.O.I teachings, Clarence was reborn once more. This time, he took the ultimate moniker: Allah. The movement he founded became known as the Five Percent Nation. The name stemmed from one of its core beliefs: 85 percent of the world's population is ignorant, 10 percent is enlightened but opts to keep the 85 percent in ignorance for their own gains. Then there's the 5 percent who know the truth and must use it to enlighten the majority. Rather than preach the inherent wickedness of white men, Allah's message focused on the holy divinity of black people. The Nation of Islam's place in hip-hop is undeniable. But it's matched, maybe even surpassed, by the Five Percenters, a much smaller, less famous sect.

To more traditional Muslims, the Five Percenters represent a debasement of Islam. Muslims mock the notion that Allah is a backronym for "arm, leg, leg, arm, head" as it's not even an English word. Further separating the movement from other forms of Islam, Allah replaced the traditional Muslim greeting *as-Salaam-Alaikum*—or "peace be unto you"—with the simple "peace," figuring that his followers should only utter words they understand. That's just one example of Five-Percenter teaching that would eventually enter common hip-hop phraseology.

Attempts to delegitimize the Five Percenters' core beliefs sidestep the movement's broader meaning and value. Even for those who never officially signed up for the Nation of Islam or the Five Percenters, or never identified as Muslim, the lessons of black empowerment were cutting. This was new-age scripture that germinated in New York's primarily black neighborhoods just a few years before hip-hop was forged in the burning Bronx.

As Knight writes in his stellar book *The Five Percenters: Islam, Hip-Hop and the Gods of New York*, "A new Black Islam was forming on the streets, inspired by both Malcolm and Elijah but owned by neither."

AS THE FIVE PERCENTERS' FRESH DOCTRINE PERCOLATED uptown, rumors spread of a violent, anti-white gang. In his May 6, 1964 report for *The New York Times,* journalist Junius Griffin described a militant, 400-member Harlem youth collective who'd split from the Nation of Islam. "Blood Brothers," according to Griffin, is what they called themselves.

The group's notoriety had been firmly established on April 17, 1964, after a group of children on their way home from school overturned some cartons at Joe's Fruit Stand at 368 Lenox Avenue. As the kids grabbed up the spilled fruit, patrolmen tried to catch the offenders, attracting some local teens to the scene. Cops emerged from patrol cars with pistols drawn and nightsticks swinging. Residents who tried to intervene out of fear for the children's safety were beaten.

"The trouble, now known in Harlem as the Fruit Riot, set the stage for the expansion of anti-white youth gangs, some of whose members call themselves Blood Brothers," wrote Griffin on

LINE THE STREETS: THE GENESIS OF DENNIS COLES, NEW YORKER

May 29, 1964.

The riot was followed 12 days later by an attack on a couple who owned a used clothing store in Harlem. Margit Sugar was fatally stabbed, and her husband, Frank Sugar, was injured. The accused became known as the Harlem Six.

Griffin's journalism attempted to connect the dots between the Harlem Six and the Blood Brothers. Citing research from the organization Harlem Youth Opportunities Unlimited (HARYOU), he described a group of rebel Muslims forged to oppose cops. Most, the researcher said, belonged to the Fruit of Islam, the Nation's male-only paramilitary wing, with members trained in karate and judo.

Blood Brothers shared their martial arts training with packs of youths on rooftops around the area of 135th Street and Lenox. It sounds like a scene straight out of a Harlem Blaxploitation flick, or maybe a Wu-Tang Clan video.

"The Blood Brothers appear to be distinguished from other youth gangs chiefly by their intensive training in karate and judo fighting techniques," wrote Griffin. "According to members, they are organized into divisions, each division consisting of a junior and senior league. Communication among divisions is maintained by a system of runners."

Griffin's reports paint a vivid picture of guerilla units bunkered throughout Harlem, ready to spring into attack. Knight speculates that the Blood Brothers were largely overblown by the reporter to sell newspapers. Even if the group existed, it was unlikely they were as organized or well-run as Griffin suggested. Either way, the imagery is impactful. The kind of thing you could build a rap dynasty on.

Meanwhile, Allah continued to tinker with Five Percent theology. Central to the movement's legacy was the Supreme Alphabet and Supreme Mathematics—a system of interpreting letters and numbers conceived in the early days of the Five Percent Nation that allowed followers to interpret the symbology with deeper meaning. Years later, it gave rappers a wordplay playbook.

First conceived in the depths of a three-day fast by John 37X, aka Abu Shahid—Clarence 13X's great comrade and one of the Five Percenters' Elders—"Living Mathematics" turned numbers into symbolic language. Shahid would serve a short prison stint, during which Allah and confidant Brother Jimmy would alter his system, devising "Supreme Mathematics." According to Knight, Abu Shahid's influence was deleted from the text's intellectual history.

The full breakdown of the Supreme Alphabet and Supreme Mathematics is easy to find, so too much detail isn't necessary here. But, as a quick example, you'll occasionally hear RZA's name spelled out in its full majesty: Ruler Zig Zag Zig Allah.

Allah played fast and loose with the rules. Take "gun," which could be broken down as God Universe Now. That sounds righteous. But in an attempt to dissuade young followers from seeking retribution when he was shot in 1964, Allah spelled it out as God U Not.

I can see the appeal. The Supreme Alphabet allowed divinity to be found all around in a way that was deep and accessible. The message that language matters right down to the letter must have influenced hip-hop, where every well-timed syllable was key.

DENNIS COLES WOULD HANG OUT AT THE APARTMENT HE resided in with the future Ruler Zig Zag Zig Allah. The space became like a casual temple, where the pair—and other like-minded brethren—would trade their thoughts on kung fu movies, hip-hop, and Five Percent Nation philosophy.

From these potted seeds grew Wu-Tang mythology. The Clan's music was more than just four-minute cuts you could nod your head to. It was a modern-day book of knowledge—holy scripture that should be immortalized on papyrus scrolls and hidden deep in the earth, where future generations can excavate it years after current civilizations have turned to ash. The philosophy of the Wu wasn't drawn from any one source, but probably wouldn't have existed at all without the input of generations of Muslim-American thinkers.

Islam has long played a prominent role in hip-hop. The Islamic inclinations of early pioneer Afrika Bambaataa through to mid-1980s artists like Poor Righteous Teachers and Big Daddy Kane played a significant role in their artistry. By the '90s, acts like Public Enemy were openly praising Farrakhan.

In 2004, Ghostface Killah professed not to being a card-carrying member of the Five Percent Nation, but to being someone who respected their teachings. Asked by AllHipHop.com if he was a member, Ghost, after a pause, responded: "No, but I study Islam. I'm not a part of the Five Percent Nation. I always respected what the brothers spoke about, but I was never a part of it. I respect the lessons and all that. I agreed with a lot of their ideology."

Ghostface spoke of his Muslim faith to *FACT* in 2013: "I went to the mosque one day and it came to me, like, this is where I belong. I left out of that and I felt clean, I felt clean. I didn't know how to pray like the Muslims but I prayed in my heart like how I regularly would pray and did the same movements they did but when I left out of there, I felt clean, clean! I done been to church, I done been to other places and I never felt like the way I felt like when I went there. I'm a spiritual brother, I follow the signs, so if that made me feel clean leaving outta there, God is clean right?"

As someone dipping into Five Percent philosophy, Ghost's oeuvre is infused with the essence of Allah's movement. He's among the greatest rappers in history to really use language. On "Camay," when he spits "Should have left my Wis' a thousand times, maybe tonight though," Ghost evokes Five Percent philosophy. In the Supreme Alphabet, W symbolizes wisdom, or the original black woman, which the rapper uses to depict the presence of his long-term partner. Here, Ghost reveals his knowledge of Five Percent doctrine, as well as his deep appreciation for language.

Some shout outs to the Five Percenters are less subtle: "Yo, the Older God put me on to how to rock this," Ghost and Raekwon chant on "Older Gods." "Maintain 360 Lord live prosperous/ It only takes a lesson a day, just to analyze life/One time in the respectable mind."

On *Supreme Clientele*, Ghost asserted his spiritual links to Malcolm X. On "Malcolm," he references the famous shot of the leader peering from behind a curtain, AK in hand. "I'm like Malcolm out the window with the joint/Hoodied up, blood in my eye, I let two fly."

Ghost's clearest, most concise ode to his faith came on the album *Sour Soul*. "Nuggets of Wisdom" is one-verse, chorus-less scripture. He pledges himself to Allah, he who taught him positivity, to speak knowledge, wisdom, and "how to walk amongst the evil and smile in the face of death." Ghost lays out his mantra for life: read the Qu'ran, stay away from pork, and keep smiling. It's about as dedicated to faith as any track that doesn't fall within a religious rap subgenre.

The flesh and blood man who went by the name Allah didn't live to see his influence on hip-hop. He was fatally shot in June 1969. Like many prominent black leaders of the day, the identity of his killer is unknown. Although the Five Percenters faltered in the immediate aftermath of his death, the movement rebounded after new authority emerged. The group took a non-hierarchical approach to leadership, and no single person replaced Allah. The Five Percenters celebrate his birthday as a holiday.

LINE THE STREETS: THE GENESIS OF DENNIS COLES, NEW YORKER

BORN ON MAY 9, 1970, DENNIS COLES GREW UP IN STAPLETON houses, a housing project made up of six eight-story buildings deep in Shaolin. Stapleton struggled to revive itself after several decades of neglect following the building, in 1964, of the Verrazano-Narrows Bridge, which shifted the commercial development of the island to its interior. Life there was no Garden of Eden.

"Park Hill was known for fly n***as and Stapleton was known for stick-up n***as," RZA writes in *The Wu-Tang Manual*, referring to the nearby neighborhood where Method Man, Raekwon, U-God, Inspectah Deck, and Cappadonna all hail from. "Park Hill n***as will shoot you, but Stapleton n***as will rob you and beat the shit out of you. A Park Hill n***a will pull up in a Benz, get out looking good, and pull a gun out. A Stapleton n***a will walk up to you with a fucking tank top and a doorag on and fuck you up. It's better to get jacked by a Park Hill n***a because a Stapleton n***a gonna whup your ass, too."

When it comes to the origin story, who can truly decipher fact from fiction? Ghost's definitive biography has yet to be laid out, and maybe it never will be. One of the clearest depictions we have comes on his solo debut single, "All That I Got Is You"—a tribute to his mother. Over the soulful groove, Ghost sketches a picture of his youth: eggs and grits for dinner, no coats in the winter, and cockroaches in the cereal box.

Going back in time, Coles reveals his father left him at the age of six. Raising eight children, his mother struggled with alcohol addiction and relied on welfare for support. The family ended up living with Coles' grandmother, aunts and cousins, 15 of them crammed into a three-bedroom apartment, sleeping four to a bed. "Things was deep," raps Ghost. "My whole youth was sharper than cleats."

Ghost's mother was also his first musical influence. She'd

spin old soul cuts at parties. The music young Dennis would hear through his bedroom wall became embedded in his blood—evident in the raw, smoky beats he's spent his career leaning towards.

On "Whip You With a Strap," from *Fishscale*, Ghost gets nostalgic about the beatings his mother dished out when he misbehaved. He sees getting whipped as a child as a sign of love, and bemoans modern parental practice that has seen spanking become less common. And, as almost an aside, Ghost briefly alludes to his mother's struggles with alcohol before breezing past as if it were nothing: "Despite the alcohol, I had a great old Mama/She famous for her slaps and to this day she's honored."

Rappers tend to infuse their lyrics with flashes of honesty wrapped in bombast. What we can be sure of is that Dennis had it worse than most other kids on the block. Two of his brothers, Dion and Davon, suffered from muscular dystrophy and, being the eldest, Dennis was often left to tend to their well-being. "Maybe I was depressed and don't even know that you're depressed," he confessed on Sacha Jenkins' documentary *Wu-Tang Clan: Of Mics and Men*.

Muscular dystrophy would eventually claim the lives of Dion and Davon. "Those is my hearts," Ghost told *The Source* in 2000. "My two brothers, man. They didn't get to run around and go do this and that or nuthin'. Not even 90 percent of the shit that I did. But when we saw each other face to face, man, it was a bond. Where I could just look at 'em and be like, 'Damn.' Start cryin' or somethin'."

Ghost continued, "Yo, man, that shit hurt. So all my albums are dedicated to my brothers, regardless, because I wish they were here to share the same things. I know everything happens for a reason. But I always ask myself, 'Goddamn, what was that reason? Why'd they have to go before I go? Or why I didn't have that."

Dennis gravitated towards rap music. The accepted genesis of hip-hop occurred when he was just three years old. In August 1973, the basement of 1520 Sedgwick Avenue witnessed DJ Kool Herc extend the percussion break by playing a second copy of the same record on one turntable as soon as the break had finished on the other deck. In doing so, Herc gifted the world the concept of the breakbeat. That's the source. From there, a galaxy of old school gods emerged.

Ghostface Killah shares DNA with dozens of the greats: LL Cool J, Rakim, KRS-One, Big Daddy Kane, and Kool G Rap in particular come to mind. If I had to pick out one who seemed to have a deep impact on young Dennis, though, I'd choose Slick Rick, with all the magnificence of his vivid storytelling and dexterous flow.

MC Ricky D might be able to walk down Broadway these days without being troubled, but his handprints are all over contemporary rap sounds. His debut album, *The Great Adventures of Slick Rick*, plays like an encyclopedia of the genre. Just one example? Jay-Z basically opens *The Blueprint* with a remake of "The Ruler's Back." That Rick anonymously lent vocals to "Girls, Girls, Girls" on the same record affirms his oft-overlooked standing. Still, just about every critic noticed when Snoop Dogg borrowed Rick's cadence step-for-step on Kendrick Lamar's 2015 track "Institutionalized." And, as an influence on Ghostface Killah, Slick Rick can't be ignored. "I kicked down doors to show that hip-hop has matured," Rick is credited as once saying. "And it may be a little controversial."

Rick rapped back and forth to himself as early as 1988, something Biggie famously unleashed on "Gimme the Loot", and something Ghost leaned on regularly. Capable of using his words and flow to construct fully functioning narratives that rippled with character and humor, Rick's position as rap's greatest storyteller is practically unchallenged.

From "Children's Story": "The cop grabbed his arm, he started acting erratic/He said, 'Keep still, boy, no need for static'/Punched him in his belly and he gave him a slap/But little did he know the lil' boy was strapped."

How do you compete with writing of such clarity? It's impossible to envision how a track like Ghost's "Shakey Dog" could exist without The Ruler leading the way.

Ghostface crystalized his links to Rick on 2001 song "The Sun," which features the pair, as well as Raekwon and RZA. Ghost is awoken at the start of the track, which may or may not be intended as an inverse to Rick's nighttime tuck-in classic "Children's Story." From there, he does what maybe too few of us do: shows love and gives thanks to that perfect sphere of hot plasma in the sky that gives us life. Even within the fine margins of writing about something like the sun, Rick's use of language is incredible. He celebrates sunshine on a relatable level ("Isn't it cool how it spreads joy, hons lay in it/And it's hard to go back to work, when your lunch break's finished") before adding a spiritual slant ("Souls have to go through the sun to reach Heaven... It's a peephole, which leads to the firmament above us"). RZA's short section is a little choppy, but the chemistry all around is pretty good.

Like Rick's street-level narratives, a sense of hometown loyalty was woven right into the Wu-Tang Clan's output. The late-1980s and early-'90s had seen the center of the hip-hop universe shift from its East Coast spiritual holy land to the Wild West. *Enter the Wu-Tang (36 Chambers)* was a huge artillery shell that helped redress the balance.

On "7th Chamber," Ghost drops us into the depths of Shaolin. "Word life, God. You know Shameek from fuckin' 212, God?" he raps, referencing building 212 in Stapleton Houses (Coles grew up in building 218). "The n***a just got bucked." From there, Ghost moves into Five Percenter dogma: "Word is bond, I'm comin' to get my Culture Cipher, God."

Still in his early-20s, Ghost's writing captured a facet of New York you won't see on a 75-cent postcard copped in a Midtown bookstore. The legend of the Ghostface Killah is doused in mythos, but could only be forged in harsh realities—brought up in the cold city of Shaolin, speaking language formulated to empower the city's oft-forgotten.

It's fitting that Staten Island has been blessed with an official Wu-Tang District. Far more than a plaque or even a statue, the renaming of the Park Hill neighborhood in 2019 officially crystallised the history the band of rappers had spent the previous 25 years forging. "I never saw this day coming," Ghostface Killah told the community members who came out to honor the Clan at the unveiling of the new street sign. "I knew we were some ill emcees, but I didn't know that it'd take it this far."

The Clan's music was like a knuckle-duster jab to the mouth. This was the bleakest vision of a city that has always blurred the lines between grit and beauty. When the cassette tape rolls through your stereo, or your compact disc whirls into life, you instantly understand New York. Once *Enter the Wu-Tang (36 Chambers)* hit the streets, they were cast in a whole new hue.

FAST LIFE

*"Like Ghostface this, Ghostface that/Ghost sold crack,
now his revelations spoken through rap."*

WHEN CONSIDERING THE HISTORY OF THE WU-TANG CLAN, fact and fiction are often indivisible. Writing their own deep mythology was one of the group's most potent weapons. The Holy Nine invented dozens and dozens of alter egos for themselves, and dreamed up an alternate image of New York to act as a backdrop for devilish adventures. In this saga, disentangling reality from invention can be akin to filling a cup with hot and cold water and then trying to separate the two.

Bios are the skin of an artist. Details and dates may provide only a limited amount of context when considering a body of work but, before we dive any further into his artistry, charting Ghostface Killah's path on Earth is still a worthwhile exercise. Let's go through his biography, then, for additional context.

Providing a dose of reality is no easy task. Ghost's legacy ranks among the most important in East Coast rap music, yet his story remains strangely elusive. The rapper's shadow looms over virtually all rap that has come out of New York since his emergence, from 50 Cent to Westside Gunn, yet there is no major biography, no dedicated documentary, nothing that considers the full sweep of his life.

Building the biography of Dennis Coles requires surgical precision. This is, in part, due to him being wildly unpredictable in interviews. For sure, he's a gripping conversationalist. His tête-à-têtes with journalists are always captivating. And you do, occasionally, even get a shot of personal information or a moment of vulnerability. Ghost just isn't a heart-on-sleeve kind of guy and probably never will be.

The intro to *The Pretty Toney Album* actually gives a pretty accurate depiction of Ghost fulfilling media obligations. Featuring a mock press conference akin to the kind a basketball player might take part in before the NBA finals, he fields questions from a room full of reporters. His response to the first totally normal query is, "It's none of your fuckin' business, man." Fair enough. But listen to the responses he gives the rest of the questions too. Dude barely answers any of them.

Here's a sample: "Yo Ghost, Ghost! This is Nina Chantel reppin' the M.I.A. I wanna know, how's the game changed since you revealed your face, man?" she asks, referencing the mask Coles once wore, ostensibly to protect his identity. And here's Ghost's answer: "The game got real, you know what I'm saying? But I'm back now, I'mma crush all that bullshit. Next question." Coherent, sure, but not exactly revealing stuff from the man behind the table full of mics.

Some years ago, I approached Ghost's people to discuss the possibility of an interview, but, for one reason or another, we couldn't get it together. For this project, I didn't seek him out to speak to. As this book primarily functions as an analysis of his work, I didn't want my partiality to be polluted by connecting with the man himself. To be clear, this is not a definitive document of Ghost's life. Such a project could only be guided by his own hand.

Laying out Ghost's biography, then, requires carving pieces of information from wherever you can find them, speculating on what he's said or rapped out being true, and separating the mythos from the truth. I'll do what I can.

THE METAMORPHOSIS OF RAP MUSIC BEGAN AMONG THE HARD bricks and cold wrought iron of Stapleton Projects. Dennis Coles' upbringing was studded with pain, prison, and poverty. Like many around him, transitioning into adulthood was fraught with titanic societal obstacles. Hurdles young men and women don't always manage to clear.

Destiny has a funny way of bonding humans who need each other's counsel. At some point in the mid-1980s, a teenage Dennis became inseparable from Robert Fitzgerald Diggs, that funky mage who—before taking up his legendary moniker, the RZA—was making moves in the local hip-hop scene under the name Rakeem. He's forever been treated as a prince of Staten Island, but RZA is actually a Brooklynite by birth and spent much of his childhood moving between the homes of his mother, father, and uncle in such faraway lands as North Carolina, Ohio, and Pittsburgh.

By 1989, Dennis and Robert were subletting a one-bedroom apartment in Stapleton Projects from the latter's mother, and it doubled as a crash pad for anybody who needed it. As many as seven people would take shelter there on any given night. Any knowledge of how groups of young men live together will tell you that it wasn't the cleanest space. Beer bottles, dead blunts, sneakers, and clothes were tossed in every corner. Kung fu flicks were screened regularly.

In his book, *Raw: My Journey Into the Wu-Tang*, U-God, a one-time resident of Park Hill, remembers evenings spent holed up in the apartment: "The nights I got tired of ducking the cops and dealing with junkies and stashing guns around where we were posted up and keeping an eye out for any potential drama that might pop up—those were the nights I'd go to RZA's place. Even though it was in Stapleton, another project just like ours, when we were at his crib, we didn't have to worry about all the shit going on back in Park Hill."

Hunger has always been a catalyst for change. Agricultural scientist Norman Borlaug once said, "You can't build a peaceful world on empty stomachs and human misery." Yet in the beginnings of the Wu revolution, food was low down on the list of priorities. According to RZA's younger brother 9th Prince, who spent some time living in the apartment, Oodles of Noodles were frequently on the menu, administering inhabitants with a diet of wheat flour, palm oil, and salt. If handed a monkey's paw and granted three wishes, the crew would probably still have eschewed sustenance for more weed and an unseen Shaw Brothers VHS.

"I remember we used to go in the store, and I'd watch Ghostface's back while he'd be stealing canned goods out of the store," 9th Prince told *The Village Voice* in 2010. "That's how bad we had it. Ghostface would throw on his big, oversized coat and just stack four or five cans in his coat pockets, and we'd walk out and shit. Times was definitely bad back then."

Prowling Park Hill at the time was Corey Woods, who'd later transform into the ice-blooded street rapper known as Raekwon. It might surprise some to hear that Ghost and Rae, two of hip-hop history's most in-tune allies, are said to have been one-time rivals. Both RZA and Popa Wu—the father of Wu affiliates ShaCronz and Free Murda, and an expert on the philosophy of the Five Percent Nation, his voice can be heard on tracks such as the Clan's "Black Jesus" and Ghost's "All That I Got Is You"—

have said as much, with the latter even claiming that Rae "used to shoot up Ghost's house. There was a big war."

The Stapleton apartment offered a sanctuary from such struggles—a small, sacred space where the stresses of the streets evaporated once you crossed the threshold and escaped into a different dimension. Right in the middle of Staten Island sat this portal to a musical nexus. The four walls served as the future Wu rappers' first studio. Over the beats that began spilling off RZA's four-track, they sharpened their blades.

In his book, U-God recalls hearing beats and smelling weed before he'd reach a front door that was never locked. "Stapleton apartments were like that," he writes. "First off, there's not much to steal, but also, who's gonna try anything up in RZA's pad with an endless cycle of hood-ass, slanging-ass, gun-toting individuals coming in and out all day?"

U-God, with a crew that often included Method Man, would arrive equipped with weed and forties (though RZA's nectar back then was Brass Monkey, a premixed cocktail of dark rum, vodka, and orange juice). "RZA and Ghost would just be in that crib all day long," writes U-God, "eatin' Oodles of Noodles, watching kung fu movies, and making beats on a little four-track recorder."

He continues, "I'd walk in and the beats would be blasting. Dudes would bring the mic cord out onto the terrace and be rhyming. Sounds fancy, but it's far from it. Like I said, the Stapleton 'jects looked like jail facilities. The terraces looked like the tiers in prison. But we'd have the mic out there, and weed be blowin', and the Brass Monkey be flowin', and everybody was just getting high and throwing darts [rapping]. It was a getaway from the drama, a way to transcend our surroundings and the day-to-day grind."

Charting an accurate depiction of how the Wu-Tang Clan was formed is akin to the historian trying to chart the story of Jesus.

There are some truths that virtually all scholars agree with: that Jesus was baptized by John the Baptist, and that he was crucified on the orders of Roman Prefect Pontius Pilate. Beyond that, there is little scholarly synchrony.

Similarly, there are some certainties in the Wu-Tang story that future historians can be sure of. There's the fact that RZA, GZA, and Ol' Dirty Bastard first attempted forming a rap unit under the umbrella of All Together Now. The group more or less fizzed out with the three cousins instead pursuing solo opportunities. The fruits of their labor manifested in two 1991 records: *Words From the Genius*, released by GZA (who was going by The Genius at the time), and RZA's EP *Ooh I Love You Rakeem*, an attempt to pitch him as a smooth loverman under the moniker Prince Rakeem. Despite the backing of Warner Bros., neither record did much and the trio's solo careers never really got going. Still, important music and business lessons were taken to heart.

Fueled by these failures, the Clan began to congeal. The story usually goes that RZA and GZA acted as the primary instigators in the forging of the collective, with Ghost not always getting his due credit. It's clear he was a key figure in those earlier days. When asked by Doctor Dre on *Yo! MTV Raps* in 1993 who the leading force who pulled the Clan together was, Method Man responded: "GZA, RZA, and Ghost." The man himself sits there in the TV studio with a mask bound to his face, which was his custom at the time.

According to RZA, "Ghost was the first to say 'That's Wu-Tang, I'm Wu-Tang.'" Whatever the case, RZA, GZA, Ol' Dirty Bastard, Method Man, Raekwon, U-God, Inspectah Deck, Masta Killa, and Ghostface Killah came together under the W.

Yet chaos and disorder continued to stalk Dennis Coles. A 2013 interview with *Crack* magazine describes Ghost in those early Clan days as "a permanently drunk, coke sniffing 'dust head' (his own term), a fearless brawler who was prone to feuds and especially unpopular with nightclub staff."

There was at least one incident that almost stole Ghost from this mortal coil before he had a chance to reveal himself to the world. In 1993, the Wu-Tang Clan were living in Ohio, awaiting the release of their first LP, when Ghost was reportedly shot in the neck and arm. Details on the incident are a little sketchy but Ghost does appear to reference the incident on "Can It Be All So Simple (Remix)," from Raekwon's *Only Built 4 Cuban Linx*: "Stumbling, holding my neck to the God's rest/Opened flesh burgundy blood colored my Guess." In an alternative timeline, the story of Ghostface Killah ends right there, and 1990s hip-hop is a lot less compelling.

Ghost neatly summarized his pre-fame life in an interview with AV Club in 2006. Asked what his life was like before the Wu-Tang Clan, he responded: "I don't know. I was just like any other street n***a. I was robbing n***as, knocking n***as out, shooting n***as. That's how it was before Wu-Tang Clan. I'll do it again if I got to."

Even in fame, the rapper endured run-ins with the law. He spent stints on Rikers Island in the '90s on a variety of charges. In 1999, he even had to step from behind prison bars, where he was serving six months for attempted robbery, to answer separate charges of criminal possession of a handgun and a bulletproof vest related to a 1997 incident when he, in one of three cars riding through Harlem, was pulled over for a traffic violation. Police claimed Ghost got out of his car and became verbally abusive.

Maybe his life outside the studio walls was racked with friction, but it was Ghost who helped put up the money to record the Wu-Tang Clan's first single, the independently released "Protect Ya Neck/"After the Laughter Comes Tears." There are a lot of accounts of how the single was financed. In 2011, Method

Man told *Complex* that, "Everybody that showed up with $100 got on the record." According to RZA's book *The Wu-Tang Manual*, it was $50 each, and for every head that didn't have the cash to throw down, Ghost made up the shortfall.

Whatever the case, "After the Laughter Comes Tears" featured verses from just RZA and Ghost, with the pair spitting over an old Wendy Rene sample. The song has become a bit of a Wu oddity to casual fans but a re-tooled version would later become "Tearz."

"Protect Ya Neck," the Clan's first posse cut, encapsulates their rusty brilliance. RZA lines up a durable boom-bap drum loop and bassline that's sooty to the touch, forming a beat that's grainy and sinister. Squad members swarm like locusts unleashed on Biblical Egypt, passing the mic like it's a hot potato before disappearing back into the shadows. The wordplay is dense and dirty, the slimy lyrics referencing "Smokin'" Joe Frazier, Arnold Schwarzenegger, and *Fame*. There's no hook, but there sure is audio snatched from a martial arts movie. As an origin point, "Protect Ya Neck" is one hell of a way to start a dynasty.

AS LONG AS THERE HAS BEEN ART, CREATORS HAVE BEEN forced to deal with the fallout. Michelangelo attacked his piece *The Deposition* after eight years' work. D'Angelo bore his torso in the video for "Untitled" before collapsing under unwanted attention and withdrawing from the public's gaze. The lesson is that you can't change the world without leaving a mark on your soul. For the Clan, the world they inhabited was simultaneously about to shrink and grow. They took to the attention like fire to kindling.

Rap values entrepreneurship and business savvy. I don't have to tell you that from 1990s hip-hop grew some of the predominant figures in 21st-century entertainment. Puffy, Jay-Z, Dr. Dre—they rode beats 'n' rhymes to the highest peaks of the American Dream. Even among the billion dollar deals, what happened next in the Wu saga is the stuff of hip-hop business lore.

After "Protect Ya Neck" sold by the bucket-load, RZA turned down record labels offering larger advances to ink a deal with Loud Records that did not include a standard clause requiring members of the group to release solo albums with the company. This allowed the Clan to strike solo deals with other labels. From there, RZA formed his meticulous five-year plan: two group albums would bookend a clutch of solo records, all of which would be produced primarily by Rakeem himself, feature heavy Clan presence, and fit the same aesthetic. Out came the Wu's debut, *Enter the Wu-Tang (36 Chambers)*, on November 9, 1993. With a flicker of their blades, Ghostface Killah and his eight brethren shifted the tectonic plates of rap from under their own feet.

In an era when hip-hop's powerbase had been extradited to the West Coast—where the melodic grooves and buzzing synths of G-funk were scoring a pop culture reckoning—the Wu made bitterly cold gangster rap cut with Five Percent philosophy and kung fu movie folklore. The Clan were immediately woven into the cultural fabric of America. You couldn't stamp the W symbol on a record without it being a huge hit.

(In a 2011 interview with Tim Westwood, even Ghost seemed surprised by the Wu's cultural reach, referencing all the times he'd seen fans with the W symbol inked on their skin. "I don't even got [a Wu-Tang tattoo]," he exclaimed. "I don't got shit on me. No ink. But these motherfuckers got it. And they gonna be 80 and 90 years old in wheelchairs, 'Holy shit. Look at Bob over here with ... the wrinkly Wu tattoo!'")

The presence of the song "Method Man" on the group's debut had solidified the perception that he was a star in waiting. And so, naturally, Meth was the first to launch out of the 36 Chambers as a solo artist with his album *Tical*. ODB followed with *Return to the 36 Chambers: The Dirty Version*. With both heralded as classics, RZA's masterplan was looking like the greatest scheme to come out of New York since the Knicks traded Mike Riordan, Dave Stallworth and cash for Earl Monroe.

Ghost was kept busy during this period. After the Wu's record dropped, Raekwon immediately got busy on his debut album, with Ghost as a key lieutenant in his vision. The pair were both drawn to a similar sonic ethos—"street shit," as Ghost called it—so even within the Clan's inner workings, it was natural that they moved together. Such was their bond that the summer of 1994 saw the dastardly duo decamp to Barbados to work on what would become Raekwon's classic *Only Built 4 Cuban Linx*. They were promptly kicked out of town.

"I'd wanted to go there because I'd seen the brochure and I was like 'Yo, this shit look nice!' But it was just weird over there man. I think the British run that shit over there", Ghost told *Crack*. "The maids who worked in the hotel—I mean, they was black—but they was just rattin' on us for no reason. They said we were making too much noise. And then we had our fatigues on, they said we couldn't even wear fatigues! Like how come you can't wear fatigues in Barbados?! They just kept fucking with us, they wanted us out of there... I remember now, it was the Royal Pavilion, those are the ones who kicked us out. But that was the best thing they could have done to us, because we went straight to Miami and that's where we got it in, then RZA recorded us right after."

If following *Only Built 4 Cuban Linx* wasn't enough pressure for Ghostface, GZA's stunning masterpiece *Liquid Swords* set the bar to celestial levels. Brutally, the preparation of Ghost's first album, *Ironman*, was marred by an unexpected deterioration of his health. He was losing weight. His mouth was dry and his vision was inexplicably blurred. The diagnosis came back: Dennis Coles had diabetes.

"I didn't know what that shit was," he told Blackdoctor.org in 2016. "The doctors in Staten Island didn't detect it, so I went to Long Island and they came up with the diabetic shit. My sugar was mad high, like 500 and change, but it was a little relief to know what it was."

Speaking to David Ma for *Wax Poetics*, Ghost remembered getting the phone call confirming he had the condition. "Dog, it was rough, you know? I mean, I was only 20-something then," he recalled. "All kinds of other shit was going on too, like my best friend got locked up. Everything started to change. I had to live different, you know? That's why the album's like that. It's dark-sounding."

Out of the pain, *Ironman* went platinum—the only Ghostface Killah album to do so.

He might have shared the cover with Raekwon and Cappadona but *Ironman* is undeniably Ghostface Killah's first long-form exposition. Even with RZA behind the boards on all but one song—and despite Ghost's later assertions that the album is "dark-sounding"—this is music lighter in tone than previously served by the Wu. For sure, it's hard to picture the album's warm soul samples on *Enter the Wu-Tang (36 Chambers)*— "After the Smoke is Clear" finds Ghost teaming up with the Delphonics over a sample of Jimmy Ruffin's "What Becomes of the Broken Hearted." And there's no way the crew rap showcase "Winter Warz" would have fit onto *Liquid Swords*.

Ironman features the sharp narratives, the wicked flashes of humor, and the soulful orchestration that would define Ghost's oeuvre. Even working within the margins of RZA's five-year plan, his individualism comes through with diamond clarity.

Eight months after the release of *Ironman* and out of the chamber came *Wu-Tang Forever*, the second album under the Clan's banner, a chart-topper, and completion of RZA's five-year plan. To further the record's commercial potential, the Clan went on a national tour with Rage Against The Machine, opening them up to a whole new audience. But there was a hitch: the crew were also booked to headline Hot 97's Summer Jam at the Meadowlands Arena in New Jersey.

"The deal was, as far as I remember, you gotta come back and do this Hot 97 Summer Jam or we're not gonna play any more of your records on your station," remembered Inspectah Deck in *Wu-Tang Clan: Of Mics and Men*. And so the Clan was forced to fly to the East Coast on their own money to play a gig that wouldn't provide a paycheck.

Enraged at the station, Ghost opted to vent on the Summer Jam stage. "Fuck Hot 97!" he screamed. "Fuck Hot 97!" the crowd responded. The Wu Tang Clan's penance for this discretion? Hot 97 wouldn't play their records for about a decade. From there, cracks started to appear. Not every group member had been sold on the idea of touring with Rage in the first place. With tensions simmering, the Clan stopped showing up to the shows.

Ghost's post-*Wu-Tang Forever* movements aren't so clear. He appeared to live almost a nomadic existence, the kind of life *Pulp Fiction's* Jules Winnfield envisioned for himself after coming face-to-face with his mortality: walking the Earth. With the tour now off the scheduled, he absconded to Africa.

Cursed by diabetes and desperate for relief, Ghost sought the help of a Beninese bush doctor recommended to him by a herbalist in Staten Island. Moving to the doctor's village, miles from any city, Iron Man was holed up in a place with no running water, where people lived in mud huts and slept on the floor. Needless to say, it was a transformative experience. When he came to meet the visiting RZA in the crowded city of Cotonou, Ghost was wearing an African dashiki, his hair had grown out, and he boasted a triumphant beard. In his book *The Tao of*

Wu, RZA remembers locals ignoring the inconspicuous Ghost, instead flocking to Rakeem himself—the man decked out in hip-hop threads. Back in the village, Ghost, RZA, and the bush doctor sat in the only hut with a TV and VCR, watching kung fu movie *Blades of Fury* as all the children in the village stood outside, peering at the on-screen action through a window.

"I seen how people was living, and how white people ran everything over there. It was fucked up," Ghost later told Jon Caramanica for the now-defunct *Boston Phoenix*. "That's the best place I ever been in my life, regardless of how the situation was, because I lived with them. I shit and pissed where they pissed. I made it my home. I'm one of them brothers, I'll fuck around and get a crib in Africa somewhere and just feed the babies all my fucking life. I give that back to God. I got a blessing with God-given talent, and I got to give it back. That's my sacrifice."

In Benin, Ghost passed the time by penning page after page of new lyrics. By the time he had surfaced back in America to prepare his second record, though, he found the Wu brand in poor condition.

It's easy to forget how desperately the Clan needed a hit in the early days of the new millennium. Many of the second batch Wu-Tang solo records that landed in the late '90s—such as Meth's *Tical 2000: Judgement Day*, GZA's *Beneath the Surface*, and ODB's *N***a Please*—were comedowns from the classic debuts that preceded them. So, like a rap game Greg Jennings, Ghost put the team on his back. The result was *Supreme Clientele*, a masterpiece.

What to say about *Supreme Clientele* after all these years and 1,000 spins? To ponder the record feels akin to writing about an ancient Greek epic or holy book. It's easy to rhapsodize over every bar, every sonic nugget, treasuring each thread in this magnificently weaved velvet drapery. Less straightforward is defining what it all adds up to. So let's start with the nuts and bolts. Once again, RZA served as executive producer, cooking up most of the beats and generally overseeing the instrumental end of the operation. Yet his shadow doesn't quite loom over the project like it does on most Abbott-led Clan full-lengths. When RZA's voice appears, he sounds like a guest and not a co-pilot. This is partially due to the mild evolution of the Wu aesthetic. A track like "One," with its propulsive piano chords, wouldn't quite have sounded right on any group record. But mostly, it's down to how Ghost prints himself onto everything around him. It could have been the blueprint for how to impose your own personality onto RZA's musical proclivities, but no Clan member was able to do it quite this well again.

The beats have a wild, experimental slant. Unlike the comforting soul of *Ironman,* the samples on *Supreme Clientele* are dark and extremely out-there. Going deep into the archives to mine new loops wasn't even always necessary: crew joint "Buck 50" utilizes Baby Huey's "Hard Times," a standard in any self-respecting crate digger's arsenal, harnessed here by RZA into a song of relentless energy with a sense of tension that is never released. (Ghost hardly tries to soothe the number either, spitting Mary Poppins' famous catchphrase frontwards and backwards—"Super-cali-fragi-listic-expi-ali-docious/Docious-ali-expi-fragi-listic-cali-super"—because why the hell not?)

There's a rain-drenched, urban bohemia atmosphere to the record. To hit play is to tumble into an alternate vision of New York, a mix of the Wu's sketch of Shaolin and the few stages of a *Streets of Rage* game. "Nutmeg" even ends with Ghost evoking the melody from Bill Withers' "Ain't No Sunshine," shouting out Brooklyn, Queens, Shaolin, the Bronx, New Jersey, and Long Island, each separated with cries of "I know, I know, I know, I know." Turns out he's the best unifier since Qin Shi Huangdi.

It's not just the immaculate front-to-back production job. Most of all, Ghost just raps his ass off. See how he makes the severe "Stroke of Death" bend to his will. Or softens his voice to the lip-gloss-bright orchestration of "Cherchez LaGhost." Over the opulent strings of "We Made It," Ghost name-drops high-end brands and describes being swarmed by groupies at the Mirage. "Nutmeg" has enough detail to fill a novella, its complex rhyme patterns built out of clusters of words that have no business being put together. (Have fun unpacking the references in lyrics like, "Swing the John McEnroe, rap rock'n'roll/Ty-D-Bol, gung-ho pro, Starsky with the gumsole"). It showcases a level of lyrical dexterity I have no hesitation calling super-human. Chris Rock might have called "Stroke of Death" "so gangster it makes you wanna stab your babysitter," but *Supreme Clientele* is not a gangster rap record. It rarely deals overtly with violence or criminality. Rather, it's Ghost unfiltered. The bottom of his soul became accessible in Africa, and he probed and preserved it; isolated it on wax for all time.

Ghost quickly followed up *Supreme Clientele* with *Bulletproof Wallets*, a more romantic, soul-driven record. By this point, the Clan were pulling in different directions. They still made good albums together—*The W* (2000) and *Iron Flag* (2001) deserve respect—but the hype around their music began to fade while their interests veered into other realms. ODB died in 2004, shattering the classic line-up and perhaps signifying the true end of the Clan's best era.

As a solo artist, though, Ghost was exploring new dimensions. While Method Man strutted the set of *The Wire*, RZA tinkered about with film scores, and GZA's output slowed to a trickle, Ghost nailed down his solo aesthetic by working relentlessly. Soul-drenched orchestration, narration-heavy lyrics, and offbeat humor—there is a Ghostface style as much as there is a Wu-

Tang Clan style. The two frequently intertwine, but do exist as separate entities.

Perhaps more so than any other Wu-Tang rapper, Ghost was embraced by online music journalism and blogging, which were usurping magazines like *The Source*—long supportive of the Clan—as the heavyweight voices of rap music criticism. *The Pretty Toney Album* (Ghost's first album on Def Jam) picked up an 8.2 at Pitchfork in 2004; *Fishscale* achieved the site's Best New Music status two years later.

More Fish, The Big Doe Rehab, Ghostdini: Wizard of Poetry in Emerald City, and *Apollo Kids* followed, completing Ghost's stint on Def Jam and, for me, signaling the end of his peak. It's been a while since he dropped a classic, though *Sour Soul* is decent. His long-discussed joint album with MF DOOM has yet to materialize.

Still, as heavy as Ghost's shadow looms over hip-hop, he has never infiltrated the mainstream as a solo artist. Only two of his singles have entered the Billboard Hot 100: "Cherchez LaGhost" and "Back Like That," which peaked at 98 and 61 respectively. His best performing single in the UK was his first—"All That I Got Is You" reached number 11.

Asserting his role as a leader, Ghost formed Theodore Unit. The group's origins can be heard on the *Bulletproof Wallets* track "Theodore," which featured assists from Trife Da God and T.W.I.Z. The crew always felt somewhat stitched together, with seemingly few supporting members staying in the group's orbit for any consistent stretch. Still, they put out the 2004 album *718*, with Ghost and Trife doing most of the heavy lifting.

Ghost is the father of 1,000 styles, we know, but he's also fathered living, breathing creatives. The tracks "Miguel Sanchez" and "Street Opera" from *More Fish* feature assists from Sun God, Ghost's son. He's got a second rapping offspring in younger son Supreme. And there is singer, actor, dancer and model Infinite

Coles. Born at the height of the Clan's popularity, the openly gay Infinite has talked about the group's use of homophobic slurs causing a rift between him and his father—a rift that, he told *Nylon* in 2017, both sides were committed to closing.

In my mind, if there's one surprise in this epic saga, it's that, despite an affinity for movies, Ghost has never attempted to cross over into a serious on-screen career. U-God does have a great story from 1996, though. In Los Angeles to record *Wu-Tang Forever*, the entire Wu-Tang Clan was invited to a party at Hollywood director-producer Brett Ratner's Beverley Hills mansion. So U-God and Ghost head to the $3.6 million home of the man who'd go on to make three *Rush Hour* movies. "We threw a gallon of rum in us," U-God writes, "I was smoking. Ghost didn't smoke, he just drank. We were pissy fucking drunk." Before they know it, U-God is threatening to punch Leonardo DiCaprio in the face and Ghost is pissing on the floor and tearing up the flowerbeds outside.

That's Ghost—his life has been nothing if not a strange odyssey. He's the guy who destroys a Hollywood player's garden arrangements, and moves to parts of the world with no running water for medical treatment. Ghost is the guy who wears opulent bathrobes to major interviews and who, in an oversized coat and white beanie hat, once gave a lecture to camera on how to survive on a $5 budget. There was Ghost, of all people, appearing on *Couples Therapy* with his partner Kelsey Nykole. He's a man of unlimited crazy stories.

Behind the art, a life has been well lived. It's his on-wax achievements, though, that will astound future generations until this planet spins off its axis and plunges into the sun. Ghostface Killah's body of work could take that long to fully unpack.

GHOST CINEMA

"Big ratchets, smoke cigars like a Bogart classic."

THE MYSTERY OF CHESS BOXING TAKES THE CLASSIC REVENGE flick outline, sheds it of any excess weight, and throws what's left into the meat grinder. It's a movie where both hero and villain are out for retribution—two powerful martial arts entities on a collision course to make Jay-Z and Linkin Park's impact feel like a mild ping.

Here's the outline: Aspiring kung fu student Ah Pao vows revenge on the man who killed his father. As Pao trains, that villain—mythically known as the Ghost Faced Killer—walks the earth, destroying all enemies with his powerful Five Elements fighting style. Each victim's bloody, defeated body is left to lie next to a ghostly red metal face. A chilling calling card tossed into the dirt by a callous killer before he moves on to his next victim.

Picture young Dennis Coles, perched on the edge of a well-worn seat in a crumbling Times Square cinema, taking it all in. Of course he was drawn to the Ghost Faced Killer. The silver-haired phenom is one of the baddest villains to ever grace the big screen.

Ghostface Killah is the greatest storyteller in rap history. He plays writer, actor, and director in his own mini flicks. His words paint pictures. His mind moves in arcs and narratives with verve so cinematic it must have been partially formed by the hours of cracked, dusty celluloid he came up on.

With Staten Island at its center, the northernmost point of the Wu-verse was those Times Square grindhouses where the Clan copped all kinds of dangerous and forbidden mythology. I picture young Ghost's bedroom being a tomb of stacked VHS tapes gathering dust in every corner. *The Mystery of Chess Boxing* (released in 1979 and sometimes known as *Ninja Checkmate*) cracked and twisted from play after play.

In "Da Mystery of Chessboxin'," from *Enter the Wu-Tang (36 Chambers)*, the Clan lean heavily on classic martial arts imagery. Like the opening of the movie that inspired its title, the music video takes place on a huge chessboard. It's the track where the Ol' Dirty Bastard formally introduces the Ghostface Killah. "No one could get iller," O.D.B. spits. Starks himself springs out of the gate: "Half-mastered-ass-style mad ruff task/When I struck I had on Timbs and a black mask." It's that crack-your-ribs street rap style mixed with kung fu mysticism that made it feel as dangerous as that spectral effigy the Ghost Faced Killer left in the soil.

Hip-hop and movies will forever be entangled. They go together like Kool G Rap and DJ Polo, or rum and Coke. Sometimes it feels like *Scarface* influenced 82 percent of all hip-hop songs. Mafioso rap took more from movie depictions of gangsters than actual gangsters. Many rappers have been lost to the film industry, spending less time in the studio as they've fawned over scripts.

Ghost's taste in movies stretched beyond the rap canon. His discography incorporates everything from Oscar winners to grindhouse horrors, from mystical martial arts joints set in

Shanghai to gritty Blaxploitation movies cut in Harlem. In an industry where "real" is a valuable currency, Ghost has never hidden his love for fiction. The movies he watched in his living room were as important a component of his artistry as the neighborhood outside his window. You don't absorb so many hours of media without it having a deep impact.

A SHAOLIN MONK MUST DEDICATE HIMSELF ENTIRELY TO A philosophy of life that has stood for thousands of years. The monks have a strict code of conduct that follows the core principles of Buddhism—self-restraint, balance, harmony with nature, and martial arts. In a world of Happy Meal heroes, there's a temptation to believe that through training and dedication you could actually make yourself fly like Zhang Ziyi in *Crouching Tiger, Hidden Dragon*. If you're going to fly, though, you need to wear robes. Otherwise, why even bother?

Rap, on its surface, doesn't value such self-sacrifice. It's immediate, garish, and materialistic. In *The 36th Chamber of Shaolin* (1978), it takes Gordon Liu's character San Te seven years to master the Shaolin Temple's kung fu secrets and re-enter the world. Conversely, rap history is full of young men and women who arrived close to or fully formed. Development can be traced not in private grottos away from view, but on tapes copped out of a trunk or uploaded to Datpiff.

The Wu Tang Clan's embrace of Asian culture and kung fu mythology set them apart from their contemporaries. It gave the Clan a barbed aesthetic, and added mystique. It wasn't just window dressing. The membership found themes in the movies that resonated deeply. On their records, dialogue snatched from films seemed to fill in as their collective internal voice. Kung fu flicks mixed Buddhist texts with ass-kickings, both of which appealed to the Wu. The Clan could drop you on your head in the streets, but they'd probably retire to someplace quiet afterwards for meditation—the gentle balancing the hard, returning their universe to its center.

In his interview with *Wax Poetics* back in 2015, Ghost explained why he took on the Ghost Faced Killer's guise: "[*Mystery of Chess Boxing* is] the one with the old dude on the cover with a white beard. People in it fronted on this character because he was out for revenge, but dude wasn't really a master yet. They killed his family and shit. So he left for 20 years and came back and caught revenge on all of 'em. I loved it. The character's name was the Ghost Faced Killer, so I took it as my identity.

"Because, back then, we was watching karate flicks, we'd get high and sometimes act shit out. Walking down the block, you'd karate chop your brother real quick, strike a pose," he added with a laugh. "I put a lot of those elements into my own songs."

RZA could talk all day about the martial arts movies he loves. "It was through these films that I was able to see and feel from a non-Western point of view," he told *Film Comment* in 2008. "Some of the dialogue struck a chord with me. It was Buddhism and psychology. 'Without wisdom, there is no gain.' There's beauty in that. And I eventually became a Shaolin disciple."

As soon as they could afford the technology, young RZA and O.D.B. were watching the movies in their own home. Three or four kung-fu flicks would role through their VCRs every day. This was the Clan's genesis: blunts, beer, movies, and making demo tapes. When they went into the studio to cut their seminal debut, drawing on those sources was the most natural thing in the world.

"My fantasy was to make a one-hour movie that people were just going to listen to," RZA said. "They would hear my movie and see it in their minds. I'd read comic books like that, with sonic effects and kung fu voices in my head. That makes it more exciting, so I try to create music in the same way."

STUDY SOME TWENTIETH-CENTURY SUCCESS STORIES AND you'll see the Shaw Brothers are right there with Walt Disney, Russell Simmons, and Beats. Forget Academy Awards fashion, the story of four siblings building an entertainment empire that would help define Asian cinema is as glamorous as it gets. The Shaws were visionaries. They were risk-takers. Even if you've never heard the name before, their influence is probably all over your favorite action hero's body of work. Quentin Tarantino, Robert Rodriguez, and RZA are among those in the West to bend the knee at the brothers' altar.

It was in 1920s Shanghai where the homophonically named Runje, Runde, Runme, and Run Run Shaw established their first film company. Their entrepreneurial father had owned one of China's first movie theatres, where lines would stretch down the street as locals turned out to see the latest Charlie Chaplin films coming out of the United States.

There was something in the movie industry, the ambitious brothers realized. Figuring that Chinese audiences would prefer to see films with Chinese stars, they invested in a camera, cut their first silent film, *Man From Shensi*, for $2,000, and raked in a six-figure profit.

Reports vary, but at some point between 1924 and 1928 Runme and Run Run Shaw travelled separately to Singapore. Living and working out of a one-bedroom apartment, the pair worked to spread their burgeoning film empire outside of the domestic market. By the early 1930s, the Shaw Brothers had a circuit of about 30 theatres under their control, and produced the first ever Cantonese talking picture, *White Gold Dragon*, in 1933.

Decades of growth and expansion couldn't be halted even by World War II, when the Shaws suffered huge property damage in Hong Kong and Singapore at the hands of the Japanese. In 1957, Run Run Shaw moved to Hong Kong to build a new studio at the city's Clear Water Bay. Dubbed "Movie Town," the facility opened in 1961 and, by the mid-1960s, it was the largest privately owned studio in the world, boasting 15 stages, two permanent sets, plenty of modern filmmaking equipment, and 1,300 employees.

Though it made all sorts of films, Shaw Brothers Studio is mostly remembered for its action-adventure movies. In 1967 the studio released *One-Armed Swordsman*, popularizing a new style of wuxia films—a genre of Chinese fiction featuring mystical warriors of ancient China—that emphasized anti-heroes and violence. The Shaws' influence was all over the genre's early-2000s revival, when films like *Crouching Tiger, Hidden Dragon*, *Hero*, and *House of Flying Daggers* hit big in both the East and West.

By 1972 the Shaws again shifted gears. *Five Fingers of Death* (also known as *King Boxer*) ditched the mysticism of the *wuxia* genre and replaced it with blood-and-bone realism. For me, it's one of the greatest movies ever made, and helped kick-start a diamond age for martial arts flicks with the Shaws positioned front and center. Rival studio Golden Harvest may have had Bruce Lee on their roster, but Shaw productions snapped and cracked off the celluloid like no cinema produced anywhere in the world at the time or since.

"The bloodiest—and possibly the most popular—movies in the world come these days not from Hollywood, London, Rome's Cinecitta or the plains of Spain," Stephen H. Y. Siu wrote in the *Montreal Gazette* in 1972. "They emanate from Hong Kong's Movie Town, a sprawling, half-real world governed by Asian film magnate Run Run Shaw."

The studio's chief liked to flaunt his success. Siu's article described Run Run's three Rolls-Royces—one gold and gray, the other two black—all of which had back seats tailored to his short stature. "Films are an art; they are also an industry," Run Run

Shaw told *Signature* magazine in 1981. "Forget that a moment and you have a money loser in your hands."

It was during this era that the Shaws produced movies that would eventually make it into Wu scripture. Joints like *The 36th Chambers of Shaolin, Shaolin and Wu Tang* (1983), *The Eight Diagram Pole Fighter* (1984), and, of course, *The Mystery of Chess Boxing* may have kicked hard, but they were underpinned by tales of rebellion, self-empowerment, and the value of self-discipline. Many starred Gordon Liu, a charismatic and athletic young martial arts star who doesn't get the credit in the West that he deserves. Think of Liu as a saintly presence every time the Clan are in the same room together. That both RZA and Liu worked on Quentin Tarantino's *Kill Bill*—RZA as a composer, Liu in the roles of both Johnny Mo and Pai Mei—was a nice moment of pop culture synthesis.

It wasn't just Ghost, RZA, and the Clan taking in these movies in 1980s New York. Black audiences have been credited with maintaining the popularity of the movies in the US. In *The Cinema of Hong Kong: History, Arts, Identity* (as cited in *China Forever: The Shaw Brothers and Diasporic Cinema*), writer David Desser argues that their appeal is rooted in the imagery of non-white characters battling their oppressors, similar to the common themes than ran through the era's Blaxploitation joints. As he points out, Hong Kong kung fu movies regularly featured an "underdog of color, often fighting against colonialist enemies, white culture, or the Japanese."

It's easy to see what drew Dennis Coles in. As Ghostface Killah, he'd later compare himself to Malcolm X, a revolutionary who, as pointed out by Sundiata Keita Cha-Jua in *China Forever*, held a "worldview that linked the darker peoples in a common political struggle against white supremacy."

Has there ever been a more iconic line of text to open a movie than that of Melvin Van Peebles' 1971 classic *Sweet Sweetback's*

Baadasssss Song? "This film is dedicated to all the brothers and sisters who've had enough of the Man." So much has been written and produced about the original Blaxploitation joint (including a 2003 movie about the movie, *Baadasssss!*, directed by and starring Van Peebles' son Mario), it's sometimes hard to view it as a piece of art itself. But what is the function of art if not to preserve what makes us human? If you wish to grapple with America in the early 1970s, watch *Sweet Sweetback's Baadasssss Song* and try to imagine a climate where a movie like this could bring the house down.

Blaxploitation was rum punch cinema. It channeled the spirit of the Black Power movement with equal parts anger and verve. *Sweet Sweetback's Baadasssss Song* became the highest grossing independent film of its time, and the studios took notice. *Shaft* (1971), *Super Fly* (1972), *Coffy* (1973), and dozens of others followed in quick succession. Cool, fashionable, powerful black heroes stood up for their race, their communities, and themselves in the face of white corruption that repressed the black community for its own selfish gains. And, of course, the soundtracks kicked hard.

Like Blaxploitation movies, a huge number of old kung fu movies focus on rebellions against authority, including a clutch of those the Clan are most associated with. In *The 36th Chamber of Shaolin*, a local uprising against the Manchu government is put down and a martial arts school sympathetic to the cause is violently crushed. One student, played by Gordon Liu, escapes to the Shaolin Temple, where he begins his martial arts training—his mind focused on returning for vengeance and liberation. By any means necessary.

Bruce Lee battles the Japanese dojo behind the poisoning of his master in *Fist of Fury* (released by Golden Harvest and known in the United States as *The Chinese Connection*). Set in early 20th century Shanghai, the movie bottles the era's tensions between China and Japan. Decades of military defeats and concessions to the Eight-Nation Alliance (of which Japan and the US were members) had weakened the great nation's international standing.

An early scene in *Fist of Fury* sees representatives of the Japanese dojo present the Chinese martial arts school with a sign that reads "Sick Man of East Asia," a historical reference deployed in the movie as a show of Japanese dominance. Later, Lee's character Chen Zhen is refused entry to a park that bears the written warning "No dogs. No Chinese." On the dog rule, they're flexible. (The scene was likely inspired by Shanghai's Huangpu Park, which was closed to Chinese people between 1890 and 1928 and, according to a popular myth, bore such a sign.) Lee quickly destroys some Japanese men goading him and smashes the sign to pieces.

Fist of Fury is remembered for its ferocious fight scenes, offering probably the ultimate showcase of Lee's unique cinematic dynamism when it came to hand-to-hand combat. But it's easy to see why black audiences were equally drawn to the story. Chen brutally dispatches all of his enemies, restoring dignity to his school and the Chinese people. He literally makes the Japanese eat their words, forcing the "Sick Man of East Asia" sign down his rivals' throats.

The film obliterates the idea of cultural supremacy and advocates the necessity of violence in taking what's yours—pride, retribution, and physical space. Like so many heroes that fight to elevate their people, Chen is eventually martyred. His death is plotted by Chinese authorities that present him to a line of armed soldiers ready to fire. In one final act of symbolic defiance, Chen sprints at the firing squad and unleashes a huge flying kick as the gunshots sound.

These heroes were Sweet Sweetback. They were Shaft. They were Coffy. They just wielded a butterfly sword or *nunchaku* instead of a double-barreled shotgun. Ghost may not have dressed in throwback playalistic garb like Ice-T, but he's always been infused with the essence of the '70s. The soulful grooves, the spirit of Black Nationalism. These were movies that smashed like a slug to the chest. They rang true to the young idealist who'd grow into a rap star, lacing his rhymes with the same vital force.

THE TITLE SETS THE TONE: *ENTER THE WU-TANG (36 chambers).* The Clan boasted nine members, each with 36 powerful hip-hop skills forged in 36 mystic chambers hidden in the belly of Shaolin. Or their mothers' living rooms, whatever. Either way, it was tutelage they would unleash on an album equal parts 1990s New York and 18th-century China. Pressing play feels like tumbling down a time portal hidden in Staten Island's deepest abandoned subway tunnels.

The first voice heard on opening track "Bring Da Ruckus" comes from a Shaw Brothers movie: "Shaolin shadowboxing and the Wu Tang sword style. If what you say is true, the Shaolin and the Wu Tang could be dangerous." It's dialogue from *Shaolin and Wu Tang* (sometimes known as *Shaolin Vs. Wu-Tang*), starring Gordon Liu, which sees a local Qing lord manipulate two rival kung fu schools into feuding with each other for his own gain. RZA probably snatched it as a perfect place-setter for the Clan's aesthetic. Yet the friction between both schools foretells the tension of the album. The rusty orchestration, concrete drum programming, and razorblade raps leave the taste of metal and blood in your mouth.

Lyrics throughout are peppered with references from Hong Kong action cinema. "Fatal flying guillotine chops off your fucking head," raps RZA on "Wu-Tang Clan Aint Nuting ta F' Wit." "Approaching me, yo out of respect, chops to neck," goes Ghost on "Wu-Tang: 7th Chamber." Who would want to start beef with nine shifus who knew this many ways to put you down for good?

Speaking to *Film Comment*, RZA laid out how the Shaw Brothers' movies directly impacted the recording of his group's debut: "I always found beauty in Gordon Liu's *Shaolin and Wu Tang*. When I heard the line, 'A game of chess is like a sword fight... you think first before you move,' I never forgot it. When we made the first Wu-Tang album in 1993, we only had VHS and it was hard to hook up your equipment to get a good sample. The dialogue bit, 'If what you say is true, the Shaolin and the Wu Tang could be dangerous' [sampled for 'Bring Da Ruckus'] was a perfect line for my crew. Another great sample, from *Five Deadly Venoms*, was, 'The Toad Style is immensely strong... it's immune to any weapon. When properly used, it's almost invisible. Raw, I'm gonna' give it you!' [used in 'Da Mystery of Chessboxin''']. Those types of intro lines were perfect for my imagination and what I wanted to represent."

The Clan's second album *Wu-Tang Forever* continued with the theme. The album's intro ends with audio from *The Shaolin Temple* (1976): "I have given it much thought. It seems, disaster must come. At best, only postponed. Shaolin kung fu, to survive, must now be taught, to more young men. We must expand, get more pupils so that the knowledge will spread." It was dialogue that served as a window into RZA's grand plan.

As forgotten as it is, the Wu-Tang Clan video game crystalized these ideas in their clearest iteration. *Wu-Tang: Shaolin Style* (known as *Wu-Tang: Taste the Pain* in some regions) plays like the Clan's teenage fantasies. The plot sees the group study under Master Xin, the last practitioner of the ancient kung-fu discipline of Wu-Tang. But when Mong Zhu, a pastiche of martial arts villains, and his Chinese warriors track Xin to Staten Island, they snatch him in the hope of discovering the secrets. It's up to Xin's students to track Zhu down and rescue their master.

The game itself plays like a mashup of *Mortal Kombat and*

Streets of Rage. It's a violent beat 'em up, all one-on-one combat, button-mashing combos, and enough blood to drown Tipper Gore. The gameplay is serviceable (as a teenager, I thought it was pretty good, though it was almost universally panned) but the project succeeds as a fully rounded depiction of the Clan's ethos. Staten Island is presented as a mystical land. There's a 36 Chambers device that takes inspiration from the classic movie. Chambers are completed by advancing through a series of challenges. You can't finish Story Mode until you have first gained 35 chambers—the 36th being awarded for defeating Mong Zhu himself.

The Clan themselves were brought to life as the fictionalized versions of themselves they'd long rapped about. Ghostface could turn himself into iron, playing on the Ironman device. Ol' Dirty Bastard's wild vocal style made him an appropriate master of drunken boxing. Plus, the soundtrack was really great. Every track was produced by RZA, including "Wu World Order," a hidden single in the group's platinum canon. Even with those boxy old PS1 graphics, the game's rusty visuals looked like the Wu's music sounded.

RZA would eventually take the natural next step on his artistic journey: filmmaking. His 2012 directorial debut *The Man with the Iron Fists* plays like a feature-length love letter to the Shaw Brothers.

AWAY FROM THE CLAN, GHOSTFACE KILLAH WAS FREE TO indulge his singular cinematic tastes without having to adhere to an overriding set of principles. A movie, in fact, acts as a preface to his whole solo career. Debut album Ironman opens with dialogue from *The Education of Sonny Carson*. Based on a true story, director Michael Campus's 1974 work explores poverty, drug abuse, police brutality, and the quest for civil rights. Its budget was small and edges were rough, but the film's power is undeniable.

Ghost snatches audio from one of the movie's most memorable scenes. An adolescent Sonny strides towards members of Brooklyn gang the Lords to deliver a message from their jailed leader, who he recently did time with. Despite being outnumbered by the irate, much older goons, a fearless Sonny asks to join the group. "I put trademarks around your fuckin' eye," he threatens in a show of strength. Primarily known for being part of a clique himself, Ghost was now looking to establish himself with his own solo display of power. As an opening paragraph to his solo career, it feels fitting. He'd revisit *The Education of Sonny Carson* again on the album.

Ghost dips into *Carlito's Way* twice on *Ironman*. Just three years old at the time, the gangster movie reunited *Scarface* director Brian DePalma and star Al Pacino for a whole new text for rappers to worship. Elsewhere, dialogue is lifted from *The Usual Suspects*, and Ghost goes all the way back to classic Hollywood on "260": "Peace Kiana, what's up with your girlfriend Wanda/She drive a cream Honda, with legs like Jane Fonda." Summoning the spirits of 1,000 movies into his work has remained one of Ghost's superpowers.

On "Cobra Clutch," from the 1998 Wu-Tang Killa Bees album *The Swarm*, Ghost dips into *Super Fly*. Taking a swing at New York radio ("Who the hypest in New York City?/Wu-Tang! Radio stop shittin' on me") Ghost asserts his NYC cred by summoning the spirit of the movie's uptown protagonist Youngblood Priest. Sampling the iconic hustler's voice, there's nothing else Ghost needs to say.

Six years after the release of his beloved sophomore album, Ghost pondered his post-*Supreme Clientele* run by fitting on the gloves of Sylvester Stallone's Rocky Balboa. "The Champ," from *Fishscale*, opens with producer Just Blaze doing a pretty good Mickey impression, comparing Ghost's previous few records—often considered to be spotty—to the hams Balboa easily dispatched before getting destroyed by Mr. T's Clubber Lang. "Remember what you first told me when I took ya in? You wanted to be a fighter. You wanted to be a killer. You wanted to be the Champ," the beatmaker screams, questioning Ghost's hunger. It lays the perfect foundation for the rapper's red-hot response.

The influence of movies doesn't always show itself in overt references. Examples of the cinematic flavor to Ghost's writing can be found everywhere. "Shakey Dog" is a masterpiece in narrative-driven writing—a one-verse, hook-free depiction of a stick-up gone wrong. The cramped backseat of a car, the smell of steak and rum, the grim violence—Ghost's relentless flow crams in enough minutiae to flood the largest cinema screen.

"Beauty Jackson," from the same album, takes its cues from classic film noir. Standing at the bus stop, Ghost spies a rare beauty. His infatuation temporarily pulls him into a black and white movie. "Her voice was a slow jam, full-length white mink/Hella fine with a beauty mark on her right cheek/When she spoke her smoke floated when it left her throat/Spelled honey when she blew it out it turned to water word."

On "Alex (Stolen Script)," from *More Fish*, Ghost tells this story about a movie writer who gets his story stolen in typical Ghost fashion. Over DOOM's '70s Sunday-afternoon drama instrumental (a sample he jacked from Henry Mancini), Starks tells a tale of filmmaking politics: "With mad options, Paramount and DreamWorks we shop it/Or Mandalay and New Line cop it/I go and get 10 mil' and blow it on the independent market." It's full mockumentary, or a film within a film. Ghost can pull his camera lens back to capture the industry itself because he's a sharp enough writer to do so.

Ghost's interest in movies reached a zenith with *Twelve Reasons to Die*. Not artistically—the record didn't see him spit the level of fire we know he can, and producer Adrian Younge's orchestration sometimes gets stuck in the mud—but thematically, it's as dedicated to a cohesive, cinematic narrative as any rap project ever conceived.

Set in the 1960s, Ghost plays Tony Starks, an enforcer for the DeLuca crime family who is murdered by his former employers after striking out on his own and falling in love with the kingpin's daughter. His remains are melted in vinyl and pressed into a dozen LPs that, when played, resurrect him as the Ghostface Killah—a supernatural force of revenge, not dissimilar to the *Mystery of Chess Boxing* character that inspired the guise.

"Basically this is a score to a vintage, Italian horror film. Obviously a full vintage horror film that takes place in 1968," Younge explained to NPR's Fresh Air radio show ahead of the LP's release. "So in my head I pictured all this artwork. All this old argental-type artwork and I wanted it to be something that Morricone could have scored back then. And then I wanted to pull in all of that Morricone sentiment. All of that old American soul sentiment. And then I wanted to kind of fabricate that in a way that the RZA would have put the album together had he been a producer in the late '60s."

RZA appears in a spoken-word role, serving as a kind of narrator. Cappadonna deserves a Best Supporting Actor nod for his role as Ghost's confidant on "The Center of Attraction," advising him to stay clear of his boss's daughter. Even in character, Ghost acknowledges his love of cinema: "My plots are like movie scripts, they well planned," he raps on "Revenge is Sweet." "Snatch you off the land and drop you off in the Sahara sand."

Ghost and Younge made a sequel. *Twelve Reasons to Die II* retread much of the same territory, though with even less replay value than its predecessor. Ghost could probably cut projects like this every weekend of the year. The album leaves an opening for a third installment. Few have been demanding it be made.

Aside from the odd cameo here and there, Ghost has never appeared motivated to follow his peers into Hollywood. Would his on-screen presence match his on-record dynamism? Maybe so, but it's probably been better for his music that the film buff in him has remained undiluted. Peering behind the curtain for too long may have stolen that purity.

The Twelve Reasons to Die projects, though, have allowed Ghost to do something that just about every person does in their own way. See enough movies and we all start viewing our life through a lens. Kids plays cops and robbers to emulate on-screen heroes and villains. Lovers propose in idyllic settings to reflect Hollywood's portrayal of romance. These motifs were undeniable cogs in Ghostface Killah's bionic make-up.

THE MASK IN THE IRON MAN

"Is it a bird? Is it a plane? (No, it's Ghost, no, it's Ghost)."

STANLEY MARTIN LIEBER WAS A HUSTLER. HE HAD TO BE. THE gangly wannabe novelist grew up in the Bronx during the Great Depression, when eviction and malnourishment were tangible risks that stalked working-class New Yorkers every day of their existence.

The child of impoverished Romanian immigrants, young Stanley's formative years were split between attending classes at DeWitt Clinton High School and working odd jobs to help his mother bring a loaf of bread or bottle of milk into the family's cramped one-bedroom apartment on University Heights. Amid the desperation, the young fantasist's escape was the literature and movies he'd drift away into. Being an actor or an author became the dream.

The Great American Novel never happened for Stanley, who would later legally change his name to its more famous form, Stan Lee. But his candid charm, steely resolve, and willingness to extend a firm middle finger to authority figures saw him enjoy the comforts of fame and fortune for over half a century. Before his death in 2018, Lee spent his twilight years serving as a mascot for the 21st century Marvel Comics machine, hugging Robert Downey Jr at film premieres, and soaking up the near cult-level adoration of fans at comic book conventions. It's a million miles away from the stifled writer who fell into an industry he never foresaw himself being a part of, just trying to squeeze a dollar out of 15 cents.

Stan Lee the celebrity has long been entangled with Stan Lee the writer. It feels like he's always been the industry's biggest name—the original rock star comic book guy who went from being appointed an assistant at the newly-formed Timely Comics (later known as Marvel) in 1939 to interim editor two years later, aged just 19. Comic books were considered artistically bankrupt prior to his emergence, but Lee insisted that the names of the creatives behind the work were a part of the Marvel brand itself, introducing to each issue not just credits, but staff news and fan letters. While it let the personality of each soft-bodied, middle-aged penciller working long hours in the Marvel bullpen shine through, more than anything it allowed Lee to use the books to cultivate his own celebrity.

On Stan's watch, comics survived German-American psychiatrist Fredric Wertham's pseudoscience, which had sparked a US Congressional inquiry into the material's negative effect on kids. He reimagined the superhero in 1960 with the Fantastic Four, transforming costumed guardians from flawless, all-American goody-goodys of the Steve Rogers ilk to petty, squabbling humans who eschewed secret identities to instead revel in their own celebrity. When watchdog group the Comics Code Authority refused to grant its seal of approval to a Spider-Man arc that addressed drug use, Lee had the story published anyway, opening the door for younger writers like Frank Miller, Neil Gaiman, and Alan Moore to introduce darker tones into the work. Put it this way: a lot of people, from the writers who followed in his footsteps to the movie execs who reimagined his characters, have gotten paid off this guy's intuition.

But Lee's legacy is simplest to gauge by listing the characters he co-created. As well as the aforementioned Spidey and the Fantastic Four, there was the Hulk, Doctor Doom, the X-Men, Thor, Daredevil, Black Panther, the Silver Surfer and, of course, Iron Man. The iron-clad superhero of the free world. America's most dramatic Avenger. And creative fuel for one Dennis Coles, who was brought into this world a borough over from Lee's Manhattan offices, just as the writer's notoriety was hyper-driving into a stratosphere not previously enjoyed by anyone working in the medium.

LESS THAN 10 MILES NORTH OF THE OLD TIMELY COMICS headquarters at McGraw Hill Building, Hell's Kitchen, lies a 102-unit apartment building in the Morris neighborhood of the Bronx that *The New York Times* would, in 2010, dub "the accepted birthplace of hip-hop." It was August 11, 1973. After spending months perfecting a new technique that involved isolating the grooves at the beginning or in the middle of a song with two turntables, a mixer and a couple copies of the same record, Clive Campbell, who will live for all eternity in rap folklore as DJ Kool Herc, unveiled his twisted creation at a back-to-school party in the rec center at 1520 Sedgwick Avenue.

Just like that, hip-hop came into the world. Herc's fiddling spawned a culture that would rock the city like a Captain America punch to the solar plexus. And, like comic books, hip-hop would fight for acceptance as a legitimate art form, infiltrate the mainstream in a big, big way, and become permanently embedded in the city's DNA. Of course comics and rap have collided throughout their gritty histories. These were two outlets of creative expression with too much in common not to intertwine.

Lee purposefully rejected the idea of dreaming up fictional cities for his characters in the way DC had homed Superman and Batman in Metropolis and Gotham City respectively. The Marvel Universe's capital has always been New York. The Stark Tower Complex and Baxter Building have become so iconic that it might shock an outsider or two to discover that the two high-rise structures don't, you know, exist. Whether gazing at Manhattan's skyscrapers from the Brooklyn boulevards where hungry young emcees have long battled for local supremacy, or from the plush Midtown corner offices where rap entrepreneurs thought out their strategy for global command in the early 2000s, you can't help but think of a swinging Spider-Man. That's the strength of the web slinger's association with his hometown.

Marvel's iconic roster—as well as that of their great rival, DC—was integrated into hip-hop mythology long before being funneled into overstuffed costumed blockbusters. Everyone from Q-Tip and Organized Konfusion to Jay-Z and Big Sean has peppered their lyrics with reference points. Others have taken it further, constructing huge parts of their bionic personas from comic's spare parts.

Underneath the twisted metal that embellishes his face, supervillain MF DOOM's mind plays like a flipbook of comic book folklore. Daniel Dumile retreated into the shadows after his brother and KMD musical partner DJ SubRoc was killed trying to cross the Long Island Expressway in 1993. Dumile spent five often-homeless years "recovering from his wounds" and swearing revenge "against the industry that so badly deformed him." What emerged from the hidden underground technodrome was rap's own evil genius, with Dumile lifting huge sections of

Marvel's malevolent warlord, Doctor Doom, to piece together his twisted ethos.

Then there's Brooklynite Jean Grae, who took on the guise of the Marvel Universe's most powerful mutant, Jean Grey. "It's a challenging name to pick," the artist formerly known as What? What? told me in 2015. If you're going to pick a character with the ability to consume an entire star, you'd better have serious powers when it comes to pushing rhymes on the mic. "Aside from being as fucking powerful as she is, there was also the idea of her story," said Grae. "Her death and rebirth."

Run throughout 1980, *The Dark Phoenix Saga* is perhaps the most famous and heralded X-Men story arc of all time. In it, telepath Grey becomes the physical manifestation of the cosmic Phoenix Force, but her transformation into an entity of pure destruction is suffocated by feelings for her Earth-based mutant squad. She might take out an entire planet, killing its population, but much of the storyline's drama comes from the battle within—your classic good-versus-evil saga. There's a sharp parallel here between Grey and Grae, the latter of whom has built an impenetrable discography by touching on everything from heartbreaking trauma to light-hearted comedy, all the while harboring the power to slay enemies with a single lash of her tongue.

Rap stars and superheroes aren't that different after all. Hip-hop has always been about empowerment, whether through providing a voice to communities gutted by decades of institutional and structural neglect, or via the accumulation of wealth that has spawned a generation of black entrepreneurs. Lee did little to mask that the X-Men were an allegory for oppression (mutants in the Marvel Universe battle systematic discrimination, the threat of violence, and legislative persecution by the government), but, in their purest form, most superhero comics are stories about repressed, powerless individuals who suddenly become unshackled from the trappings of their unremarkable human form.

Comic books resonate because they have simple themes. They deal with loss, grief, redemption, fame, and struggle—all classic takes from common rap narratives. Hip-hop was forged in the flames of the burning Bronx by kids of Jamaican immigrants. Superman, in many ways, is the ultimate immigrant. Fleeing desolation to thrive in a burgeoning US metropolis, he's the embodiment of the American dream.

Like Superman-Clark Kent, the majority of the coke rappers, gangster rappers, and other hard-as-nails hip-hop heads have clearly defined borders when it comes to compartmentalizing their personas. William Leonard Roberts II and Rick Ross. T.I. versus T.I.P. Dennis Coles, Ironman, Tony Starks and Ghostface Killah—veneers to hide the real person underneath. Or, as *Kill Bill*'s eponymous villain puts it, costumed attire donned to become one's true self.

DENNIS COLES DIDN'T GROW UP A COMIC BOOK KID. HIS WAS not a youth spent peering at the world from behind his bedroom curtain, lost in the trivial minutiae of the inner workings of the DC cosmos. Put it this way: he was no Staten Island Elijah Price, Sam Jackson's brittle Mr. Glass in M. Night Shyamalan's *Unbreakable* trilogy, the director's love letter to comics.

In his review of Ghost's 2014 album 36 Seasons for music blog *Stereogum*, critic Tom Breihan remembers meeting him on the set of the "Back Like That" video in 2006. While flicking through a copy of Marvel's *Civil War* on the sidelines, Breihan was approached by the rapper, who, decked out in the swaggering opulence of a purple bathrobe, quizzed him on his choice of reading material. "Ghost thinks [comic books are] cool, but they're not a part of his life," the writer explained.

But if Ghost didn't have radioactive venom running through his veins, he could still draw superpowers from the pulp fiction. His Wu-Tang brethren may have preached that the tongue is a sword, but Starks has always used his more like pen, pencil, and color palette, sketching out and bringing to life narratives that feel as full, rich, and snappy as those laid out by the artists and writers who dragged on Newports long into the night, staring blurry-eyed at paneled pages.

In *The Wu-Tang Manual*, RZA's guide to the influences that shaped Clan mythology, the Abbott outlines Ghost as "Iron Man, and always has been. That's because he was known as being very strong in the streets". No mention of billionaire philanthropists or genius playboys. Nothing on the eternal struggle between good and evil. On the ground-level grind, young Ghost was more concerned with metal bars than the man in the metal suit.

One of the most common elements on Earth it may be, but iron represents toughness and impenetrability. Take the Bronx's own Iron Mike Tyson. Before the end-of-career defeats that came when the long-extinguished pugilist was turning up just to pay the bills, he was the youngest ever heavyweight champion of the world, whose powers of intimidation slayed so many opponents before they even stepped into the ring. Small for a heavyweight but boasting a 20.5-inch neck, Tyson's low center of gravity and constant head movement made him very difficult to lay a glove on and provided the perfect starting position to unleash his unbelievable power. In the ring, he was like a piece of scrap iron—damn near impossible to hurt.

On the mic, Ghost displays some of the same relentless energy. His voice is solid and robust. His bottomless flow unshakeable. Sometimes he sounds more iron than man. The Wu's early sound was grim, gritty, and street-oriented. Ghostface was the cement in the mixer.

The rapper made no reference to Iron Man the character on *Enter the Wu-Tang (36 Chambers)*, but it was clear that comic books were an important element in the Clan's philosophy, right down to their assembly. More so than any group of their size, Wu-Tang felt like a conglomerate of potent individuals. Considered separately, they were nine powerful warlocks, but banded together, there was no force in the universe that wouldn't fold at their mercy. A hip-hop Justice League or Avengers.

Comics had always been around the Wu. "Hip-hop was always a youth thing and youth read comics," wrote RZA in *The Wu-Tang Manual*. A childhood spent breathing in this colorful world manifests itself in his work right from the beginning. "Yo, there's no place to hide as I step inside the room/Doctor Doom, prepare for the boom," raps RZA on "Wu-Tang Clan Aint Nuting ta F' Wit," comparing his lyrical barbs to the supervillain's explosive weaponry. RZA's heavy doctrine would become an elaborate mix of Islam, Hinduism, Buddhism, Christianity, Shaw Brothers' scripture, and the Silver Surfer. His earliest exposure to visual storytelling would later be mined in his career as a film composer and director.

"Growing up, I used to read comics like a movie," RZA wrote. "I'd make the music for it in my head, I'd see the choreography, the shots, everything—it'd take me an hour to read one, just plotting it out."

Ghost was toying with comic book mythology way back then. The first phase of his career saw the 23-year-old protect his true identity with a white hockey mask. Rumor has it that the young hustler was hiding behind the face-hugging fiberglass to evade being captured by police, but to gaze upon the featureless piece makes the truth feel so much more sinister.

"Ghostface Killah, you know what I'm sayin', he on some

'now you see me, now you don't'," growled Method Man when laying out Wu folklore on a radio interview that would become part of *Enter the Wu-Tang (36 Chambers)*. Dennis Coles was being presented as a literal ghost—maybe even a killer. That is, a loyal swordsman who could flutter in and out of the shadows before striking at will. Blurring the lines between myth and reality was his weapon. Skewering his image induced a sense of danger.

Whether there were practical concerns for Ghost to want to obscure his true self, we can't be sure. He insisted the tales of him using a mask to dodge the law were false in a 2006 interview with *Prefix*, but did concede, "Yeah, I was getting my hands dirty back then. N***a do what he do." What it did do was turn him from Bruce Wayne into rap's own Batman—an incorruptible, everlasting symbol.

Masks and costumes make it really easy to slap comic book characters onto Happy Meal boxes, but the reasoning for the headpieces pre-dates such commercialization. Heroes and villains conceal their faces to become more than just men. There is power in the symbolism. You can't hope to defeat an enemy you don't understand. And, just as hiding his features dehumanized Jason Voorhees and made him a seemingly unyielding killer, young Ghost appeared more supernatural than man—a relentless rhyming machine with powers that could be unleashed over 16 bars.

The Wu-Tang Clan made street music that sounded hard as diamond and, behind their first line of attack, evil lurked in the shadows. If you're going to wear a mask, you better bring a certain level of malevolence. Throughout *Enter the Wu-Tang (36 Chambers)*, Ghost raps like a behemoth, pitching himself as a, "Rap assassin, fast and quick to blast and hardrock," on "Wu-Tang: 7th Chamber," scorching all around and escaping into the dusk once more.

Playing the Wu's enigma has suited Ghost. On *8 Diagrams*,

he'd smash up the scenery through the record's first half and all but disappear down the stretch. He's frequently been RZA's greatest weapon, and the one he's struggled the most to control. If comic book's most prominent theme is the battle of good versus evil, then Ghost—the villain—is mirrored on the other end of the spectrum by Method Man, the Wu's most visible member in the early days. And yet the pair are also one and the same—two sides of Harvey Dent's scratched up silver dollar.

This duality runs through most comic books—the idea that Peter Parker and Spider-Man are two harmonious sides to the same person, the weak and the brawny siphoned off into two clearly defined sections of Parker's personality. But these themes are at their most tangible with Dent and his impious alter ego Two-Face, whose 50 percent acid-scarred physical form reflects an internal battle of good versus evil that can only be settled by the flip of a coin.

How would you describe your personality? Are you gregarious? Introverted? Silly? Serious? Or are you all those things, just not all the time? Comic book masks, deformities, and second selves are just an exaggerated parable for the complexities of this thing we call life—we are all a lot of different things to a lot of different people.

Ghost has used comic book tropes to exaggerate and separate distinct elements of his personality—Ghostface Killah, Tony Starks, Iron Man, Pretty Toney, and his various other disguises are all different looks that form the same impenetrable being. Whichever of Ghost's faces he straps on, what's in the trunk is just as compelling as what's painted on the hood.

Iron Man's armor has gone through a constant process of upgrading and redesign. The clunky metallic exoskeleton that helped him escape villain Wong-Chu in his comic-book origin story (in the 2008 movie, it's Afghani terrorist group the Ten

Rings) was soon thrown out for the cutting edge tech of the red and gold suit. Likewise, Ghost's hockey mask had been discarded by his solo debut, his true face becoming more defined as he used the extra space of a full-length record to establish his narrative-heavy style.

Post-*Ironman* found him falling further into Marvel iconography. *Supreme Clientele* opens with the hero's theme music from the 1966 cartoon *The Marvel Super Heroes*, and throwback Saturday morning kids' TV loops would become a common feature on his records, adding a bit of wacky flavor to his concrete street rap, or adding some neon-lit signs to point listeners to the more buried references, training the ear to pick them up.

In taking on the Iron Man-Tony Starks guise (and it's important at this stage to note the difference between Stark, Iron Man's true identity, and Starks with an "s," Dennis Cole's twisted version of the character), Ghost broke from normal rap protocol by mixing his own mythos with figures of authority. Few hip-hop artists have repped the Avengers, whose bloated membership is loaded with characters cleaner than a 21st-century Dr. Dre beat. Instead, they tend to find kinship with the persecuted, the outsiders, and the wicked—those with stories that mirror typical rap narratives.

But, while Tony Stark may be one of Marvel's most prominent heroes, he's also a deeply flawed one. The bearded billionaire is a narcissist, a womanizer, and a recovering alcoholic, and, beneath the impenetrable armor, he hides the potentially fatal weakness of a piece of shrapnel that moves ever closer to his heart. Flaws of the human condition pose a bigger threat to Iron Man than anything traversing the far reaches of the Marvel Universe. If Ghost wanted to play superhero, he was going to take on the guise of one more likely to sweat over a fifth of vodka than an intergalactic villain.

Coles, though, is less concerned with Stark's metal-encrusted hero than he is with Tony himself, taking on the moniker in the same way Biggie would sometimes go by the name Frank Wright, a revved-up alter ego that borrowed heavily from Christopher Walken's turn in the 1990 movie *King of New York*. Similarly, the lines that separate Ghostface Killah, Starks, and Iron Man blur constantly as he rotates between each costume like a rap chameleon.

Frequently referring to his Tony Starks guise in the third-person, Coles detaches himself from the street superhero he's created, taking ground-level depictions of the low-end grind and adding core tenets of the Marvel idol he so admired. So, while the one-time mechanical engineering prodigy uses his genius-level intellect and business savvy to run a company that develops and manufactures advanced weaponry and defense technologies, Starks boasts the same venerable traits, albeit displaying them less in the big business boardroom and more on the shady street corner.

But stronger than just this surface-level appropriation has been Ghost's ability to bring to life his dense narratives by weaving in comic book flavors. The Marvel Universe acts as a kind of souped-up version of our own reality, where the presence of hundreds of costumed heroes is considered the norm. Similarly, Ghost's story-led tracks often feel like a hyper-reality. Sometimes the building bricks seem straight jacked from the comic book world. It's a fantabulous vision of New York that Starks operates in—one populated with a cast born in the outer reaches of his mind.

The track "Angelz," for example, sees Ghost team up with his frequent collaborator DOOM, whose dedication to comic book legend always seems to offer added inspiration. Rapping over some opulent strings that nod and wink to the *Charlie's Angels* theme tune, Ghost recalls the tale of the "three white bitches who worked for Tony Starks," a trinity of beauties decked out in knee-high boots and Wonder Woman bracelets that he can deploy to do his dirty work. The rapper peppers the story of the trio with imagery that pops with the crash-bang-wallop of a graphic novel—all dirty skirts, beauty marks, and pointed glocks.

You can also see this applied on "Ray Gun," from Ghost's Badbadnotgood collaboration album, *Sour Soul*. The Canadian jazz group's peppy drums, leisurely strummed guitars, and playful organ chords take you on a stroll through the grubby streets of lower Manhattan. You can feel the steam coming out of the downtown sewers, where zoot-suited henchmen lay low in seedy bars and backdoor speakeasies.

"Back in black, it's your local superhero from the hood/Ironman Starks' got the good," raps Ghost, setting the scene. The superhero imagery continues with symbolism lifted straight from the pages of a couple of classics: "My Wu crescent sign's in the sky at night," a nod to Batman, of course, and "Ain't a bird or a plane, it's Ghost on the mic," where the rapper likens himself to Superman.

Similar in ethos is "Supa GFK." Rapping directly over Johnny Guitar Watson's "Superman Lover," Ghost establishes himself as no ordinary mortal, opening the track with the whispers, "Is it a bird? Is it a plane? No, it's Ghost." How the fuck can you hope to destroy a humanoid who harnesses the power of a Kryptonian? Verse one sees him gun down his enemies with ease.

It must have been an easy decision for supergroup Czarface (Wu-Tang veteran Inspectah Deck and Boston underground stars 7L & Esoteric) to tap Ghost for their 2019 joint album, *Czarface Meets Ghostface*. It had been less than a year since they'd clashed with DOOM on *Czarface Meets Metal Face,* the first installment in their comic book-inspired series, and Ghost was another perfect foil. The superhuman rappers trade blows over rusty beats throughout. On "Powers and Stuff," Ghost walks through the night with "cat-like vision," boasts about the machinery division in his own Starks Enterprise, and even drops a reference to *Battlestar Galactica*. Both *Czarface Meets* records even feature glorious album artwork, reminiscent of old Marvel covers.

Such was Ghostface's association with the Iron Man character that he was recruited to record a track for the soundtrack of the first big budget movie adaptation. The song appears in the flick but never received an official release (Ghost himself actually made a cameo as a party guest, which was left on the cutting room floor). Still, rapping from Stark's perspective, it offers some revelations into why the character does appeal to him: "Keep a few bad chicks, I ain't your average hero/Movie premieres, catch me with the zam enginero/Six six eleven gold, playboy industrialist/Face of a ghost, mind of a technologist."

Cash rules everything around Tony. Iron Man is one of the few heroes who unashamedly takes advantage of his fame, wealth, and resources to appease his most carnal desires. You don't have to dig deep to see the appeal for Ghostface Killah, who has spent his adulthood brooding in his lair, penning rap lyrics with all the impact and complexity of an advanced war machine. It's two sides of the same hustle. You get rich or die tryin'.

36 Seasons is not Ghost's best album. He never spits "Shakey Dog"-levels of fire on any track (all of which are helmed by 1970s throwback band the Revelations), and the imagery doesn't crackle and pop like on his best stuff. Still, the 2014 album represents the zenith of his interest in comic book tropes and masked mythology—a long-form love letter to the medium as a form of storytelling.

Teaming up with comic book writer Matthew Rosenberg—who not only conceived the narrative, but filled the CD booklet with some 20 pages of glorious illustrations—Ghost takes the opportunity to bite at the Iron Man mythos harder than ever before. The LP's running plot sees him inhabiting the role of a masked vigilante superhero brought back from near death as a more powerful being, using new-found strengths to pop off on his enemies. "The almighty GFK, the masked avenger/New York's top contender, city defender," he declares on "Call My Name."

All mad scientists and twisted facial features, it's your classic superhero origin tale, set in a Staten Island only known to Ghost, where metal masks and adamantium skeletons prowl the streets looking to carve out their own corners.

WHEN STAN LEE DREAMED UP IRON MAN IN 1963, IT WAS TO explore Cold War themes, particularly the role of technology and industry in the fight against communism. Throughout the character's evolution, his core tenets have been preserved while other elements change and flow to adapt to a more modern world.

More than three decades after Iron Man's first on-page appearance, Dennis Coles reimagined the character to adapt to his world. Taking the warmongering industrialist, stripping away his heroism, and boiling him down for a warped vision of the hardened boulevards of Shaolin, Ghost's stories unite America's last great art forms, adding flavors to hardcore hip-hop that most of his contemporaries can't even begin to wrap their head around.

Hero or no, Stark wanted to rule the world. Starks just wants to rule the streets.

COMFORTABLE ROBES: ON GHOSTFACE KILLAH'S MIGHTY OPUS FISHSCALE

"This is architect music, verbal street opera."

IRON MAN WAS WOUNDED. NOT EVEN ARMOR CONSTRUCTED with gold titanium alloy can withstand lashes dished out by the music industry's evilest forces. It was the mid-2000s and Ghostface Killah's solo career had suffered numerous lacerations, from frequent problems with clearing samples, to tracklisting errors, to the confusing decision to release 2004 record *The Pretty Toney Album* as just "Ghostface." It added up to a body of work that, though critically revered, included exactly zero Billboard Top 40 singles.

How many hits can a creative soul take? How heavy an anchor can the human spirit carry around its neck? So much of Ghostface Killah's early solo career was sloppily handled, he was entitled to wonder if a curse had been placed over his head for old sins. Broken down, dismayed, Ghost went over to Def Jam Records, headed up at the time by Jay-Z and battle-hardened veterans of putting out classic hip-hop records. He gave up the weed, regrouped, and, after revving up on *The Pretty Toney Album*, dropped *Fishscale* in 2006, the best album Dennis Coles knew how to make.

Though never one to go into much detail about anything behind his music, while promoting *Fishscale* Ghost alluded to his prior frustrations: "The last couple of albums really had no buzz on them—on me or my album," he admitted to the website AskMen in 2007. "You know, based on what I went through at Sony [Ghostface's previous record label] and what I just went through at Def Jam the first year in there [with the transition going on] this one seems like there is a lot more promotion: on the internet, what I'm doing out there on the streets as far as shows and all that."

He continued, "So this one... I felt it more, you know what I mean? Regardless of how the album comes out or how it turned out to be. But I just felt like a little bit more is going on; whether it's promotion, marketing or people being alert."

Fishscale is the sound of Ghostface throwing everything he had into a project. A genius at the height of his powers focused on creating a classic work. Ghost sounds unshackled—a Rottweiler released from his leash, sprinting towards a slab of meat. And though the extra layer of polish and a couple of radio-minded tracks suggest he had some notions of commercial success for the record (who really knows what's going on underneath Tony Starks' peaked beanie?), there's very little of the ring-chasing that often punctuates major label releases, when executive intervention and sales targets impose barriers on an artist's natural inclinations.

Can you imagine what those barriers might have looked like? Remember, this was 2006. Lil Jon's reign as chart king had not yet ended. 50 Cent was still around, but New York street rap was at its lowest point. Yet along came Ghostface, orbiting a gritty, *John Wick*-style version of the city, sounding distinctly like himself. The bars are dense and direct, the beats are wild and psychedelic. Play it out of context and it's a difficult album to date, mainly because the styles Ghost tinkers with feel so timeless. It's proof the rapper could glance at the Billboard charts without spiritually losing his connection to the New York concrete. *Ironman* and *Supreme Clientele* often dominate conversations on Ghost's best record but, for me, *Fishscale* is an equally impressive monster. He slays every beat, hitting enough stylistic corners to convince you he can do anything on the mic.

The title comes from the term for uncut cocaine and, though not a concept album in any meaningful sense of the word, *Fishscale* finds Ghost comfortably inhabiting his mafioso rap persona, albeit a little bit older and a little bit wiser. He's Stringer Bell—not old compared to, say, the Earth, but still one of the senior cats on the block. A hardened veteran who has seen too damn much, but not yet the piercing end of a fatal bullet.

Ghost connects past to present on opening skit "The Return of Clyde Smith (Skit)," resurrecting a character he debuted on *Supreme Clientele*. Using voice-editing software to alter his larynx into something impossibly deep, Ghost as Clyde lays out his realness remit—while referencing *Vanilla Sky*—over the beautifully caressed keys of Brother Jack McDuff's "Summer Dream." Starks' natural ridiculousness meets pretty musicality. The message is clear: nothing has changed. Yet much had changed.

Things kick off properly with "Shakey Dog," a wonder of a song produced by Lewis Parker. The little-known British musician need never touch a mixing desk again—his place in rap history was secured when he flipped Johnny Johnson and the Bandwagon's version of "Love Is Blue (L'Amour Est Bleu)" into a mean piece of uptown street drama that helps set the scene for *Fishscale*. Ghost leads us through a botched stick-up with HD-level detail, richly describing every thought that races through his mind as he approaches the door and enters the apartment where the ill-fated drama takes place. This is Starks' writing at its strongest. Check out how he spies a 70-something-year-old woman with a shopping cart in the hallways. Conversing with an associate named Frank, Ghost reveals that the woman, in a scene straight out of a mafia movie, once murdered her brother-in-law at his boss's wedding before fleeing to Venezuela. Now she's at his enemy's doorway with a shotgun. The wordplay is as knotty as it is genius. A thousand rappers must have felt like giving up after hearing it for the first time.

Yet that's just the start of it. *Fishscale* features the following: an ode to Ghost's local barbershop, a whimsical look back on childhood, two criminal associates called Dr. Glove and Woodrow the Basehead, and a beautiful woman named Dawn who is definitely not an Avon lady. Only Pretty Toney, though, could do it all while still delivering a metaphysical underwater adventure (possibly the afterlife) laden with Islamic references, as he does on "Underwater."

A song like "Kilo" connects the dots between Raekwon's two *Only Built for Cuban Linx* albums, released in 1995 and 2009. It's as perfect a coke rap song as you'll hear; the lean, 1970s-style sample carved up by producer MoSS providing a wickedly funky backdrop for the two salty kingpins to count their cash and survey their empires. "Some say a drug dealer's destiny is reaching the ki'," says Ghost. "I'd rather be the man behind the door, supplying the street." Raekwon and Ghost's chemistry in no way sounds strained.

As I've previously mentioned, "The Champ" opens with Just Blaze doing a Mickey from *Rocky* impression to criticize Ghost's last few records. "He's an animal, he's hungry," Blaze shouts, using Mickey's fears about Clubber Lang to warn about the rapper's unnamed competition. "You ain't been hungry since *Supreme Clientele*." The insinuation is that Ghost's previous two records, *Bulletproof Wallets* and *The Pretty Toney Album*, were substandard affairs. This never sat right with me. *Pretty Toney*, in particular, is classic Ghostface. Still, it laid out Stark's mentality for *Fishscale*—to get back to his most ferocious and best.

Above all, "The Champ" is a masterpiece in rap braggadocio. Ghost reminds hip-hop that his career predates Nas dropping the Nasty prefix from his name, boasts about his money clip ("Godzilla bankroll" is a particularly fun use of language), and taunts an anonymous rival childishly with a chant of "liar liar, pants on fire" before adding the particularly barbed appendix, "You burning up like David Koresh," a nod to the leader of the Branch Davidian religious sect who died in a fire when its compound in Waco, Texas, was raided and burned to the ground by the FBI in 1993 (an incident he also referred to all the way back on "Bring Da Ruckus"). The breadth of references that Ghost pulls from is forever astonishing.

With a rolodex that included the likes of Jay-Z, Usher, The Game, and T.I., producer Just Blaze was a sensible pick for a rapper hoping to drop a commercial hit in 2006, though much of the rest of *Fishscale* features beatmakers more in tune with the streets than the radio (no RZA though). Pete Rock produces two cuts while MF DOOM helms four, including the curious Wu-Tang unification record "9 Milli Bros." I say curious because RZA's contribution consists of him simply stating the names of Clan members, lifted and altered from his solo song "Fast Cars." Nor is it an original DOOM beat, instead summoned, like so many have been, from his *Special Herb* archives. And yet, despite this apparent lack of interest, "9 Milli Bros." is one of the great 21st-century Wu records, full of immediate rhyming, crew love, and undeniable on-mic chemistry.

There are also two cuts featuring J Dilla beats. Dilla died just one month before *Fishscale*'s release and three days before the release of *Donuts*, the beautiful collection of short instrumentals that defined the bohemian beatmaker's genius. *Donuts* is loaded with cuts supposedly compiled into a set because they were impossible to rap over, yet there goes Ghost, flowing gorgeously over the short, smoky, romantic "Beauty Jackson" (the instrumental was originally called "Hi") and vocal sample-heavy "Whip You With a Strap." The chemistry between Jay Dee and Ghost sizzles. It's tantalizing to think of what further collaborations between the pair might have yielded. Particularly when, in an interview with *The A.V. Club*, Ghost revealed he'd never actually shared a space with the legendary producer: "I haven't met Jay Dee. I haven't done nothing. I [just] listened to his beats. I liked them and I just wrote to them. I did it and that was it. I wished he had had a chance to hear what I did to his music."

He expanded on how the beats ended up on *Fishscale* in an interview with *Fader*: "First of all, I never met J Dilla. I got it from my man Plain Pat who's my A&R at Def Jam. His job is to find the artists beats. He brought me the CD. One day I happened to sit down and go through songs and I found that beat on there."

On the other end of the collaboration spectrum is Ne-Yo. Most rap albums from the early years of the new millennium slid R&B collaborations into the mix, and "Back Like That" is perfectly fine, with Ghost crooning about a faltering romance. In the video, he performs alongside Ne-Yo in what appears to be a purple mink coat, a neck full of garish gold chains, and a grey winter hat, so that helped justify the record's existence. Plus, the remix features Kanye West lusting over Eva Mendes and dubbing the dinner his date orders as "Kobe beef like Shaquille O'Neal." "Back Like That" was one of two singles taken off *Fishscale*—the other is the Pete Rock-produced crew jam "Be Easy," a solid jump-around record I throw on at parties when I feel like playing a Ghostface song.

That's part of *Fishscale*'s magic—hearing Ghost test himself across a range of styles, tying the album together with his peerless rapping and the indomitable force of his personality. Check out "Columbus Exchange (Skit)/Crackspot": Ghost summons a whole cast of characters to populate his drug den (even name-dropping Raekwon and Trife Da God) as he reveals his paranoia that the narcs might be closing in. Even the skits are funny. Ghost might be my favourite skit-maker in rap history. Only Cam'ron really rivals him. Both are capable of spinning their surrealism into comedy. They've got star quality and comic timing. I wouldn't cull most of the skits from their discographies.

Fishscale didn't do *Wu-Tang Forever* numbers, but it did hit number 4 on the Billboard charts—a very respectable result. More importantly, it left an oft-unappreciated legacy. It spawned *More Fish*, a fine odds-and-ends collection, while *Big Doe Rehab* felt like the unofficial continuation. As sequels go, it's not quite as good as *Fishscale*, but it follows much the same formula and is still an excellent record. *Fishscale* also set the tone for a series of dealing-focused albums that included Jay-Z's *American Gangster* and Rae's *Only Built 4 Cuban Linx... Pt. II*. These were hardened drug-rap records forged by guys who weren't kids anymore.

Mostly, though, *Fishscale* should be remembered as an uncut collection of Ghost's genius. It healed the wounds of past wars and kicked off the fruitful middle period of his career.

"This is like one of my first albums right now," he told AskMen. "Within the next couple of years—three, four, five more years—the world is going to get to see the real Ghostface Killah." And so we did.

LIFE CHANGES: 8 DIAGRAMS AND THE FRACTURING OF THE WU

"On anything that RZA throw, Ironman's invisible."

THE WU-TANG CLAN STEPPED IN THE ARENA FULLY-FORMED. There was no Year One origin story. No apprenticeships served under a powerful shifu. RZA's manifesto was complete, concrete and unbroachable. The group were like nine mythical warlocks who sprouted up from the Earth's crust perfectly constructed and began walking the cold, hard streets of New York. The lack of discernible genesis made them seem without weakness.

What we didn't see was Chambers one through 35—the seven years of exile in the Shaolin temple perfecting their craft. Hours and hours of crumbling kung fu mythology absorbed in a dilapidated Times Square theatre. A lifetime of ground-level street knowledge picked up in the provinces of Brownsville, Bed-Stuy, Park Hill, and Stapleton Projects. Countless nights bopping heads to Cold Crush Brothers, Grandmaster Flash and the Furious Five, Funky 4 + 1 and, later, Eric B & Rakim, KRS-One, Big Daddy Kane, Biz Markie, Marley Marl, and the whole Juice Crew. This was knowledge the Clan turned into wisdom. Wisdom that they turned into power.

Only staunch Staten Island loyalists copped RZA's goofy pre-Clan solo single "Ooh We Love You Rakeem," or GZA's unformed first album, *Words from the Genius*. For everyone else, the Clan's debut single "Protect Ya Neck" wasn't just a warning shot—it smashed like a spear in the chest. First album *Enter the Wu-Tang (36 Chambers)* was as complete a scroll of brass-knuckle New York hip-hop as the golden age produced. That it didn't overshadow all that's come since is a testament to the Clan's prominence and longevity. Ask Nas, who hit the highest peaks of rap stardom but, in many eyes, never truly managed to step out of *Illmatic*'s long shadow.

RZA never stopped evolving. His five-year plan for the Wu was ironclad, but his life's work boasts far more breadth. His talent led to fame. He leveraged both to work with some of the best people across both music and film. And his mind continued to grow. Too often in the history of music have we seen artists retract once they lose touch with their roots, instead dropping into the soundproof booth of fame, money, and success. The evolution of Robert Diggs saw the four corners of his creative canvas stretch out—but there was no dilution in colour as he broadened his strokes.

36 Chambers boasts the songs the Wu will likely be most remembered for, but I've treasured *8 Diagrams* as much. Released in 2007, the Wu's fifth album feels like the natural completion point of the Tao of RZA—the most complete blueprint of the deep mythology the Abbott immersed himself in and pressed onto the group's output. The kung fu dialogue is at its most dense and lengthy; the lyrics are cutting as ever. In the years since the Clan's emergence, RZA had learned to play more traditional instruments, adding a whole new set of legendary weapons to his already mighty arsenal. Musically, *8 Diagrams* is a genius at his most expressive—a concentrated tapestry of ideas with every shred of orchestration threaded with experimental flutters.

The record still sounds hard as fuck, of course—as though it was encrusted in heavy rock for 1,000 years and excavated by archaeologists seeking to find links between us and a beautiful lost civilisation. But more so than any Wu record, *8 Diagrams* feels wholly organic. The arrangements shift and change like an evolving life form. Song structure goes out the window as colors collide into a sonic smörgåsbord of scattered thoughts and hoarded ideas.

Brought up absorbing the crash, bang, and wallop of comic book legend, RZA had long been linking the sounds in his head to imagery in front of his eyes. His work as a film composer had seen him fully explore the connection between visual and audio. Building on that experience, *8 Diagrams* feels like visceral fantasy brought to life. Songs that play like Saturday morning cartoons dragged past the watershed. The record is a 35mm grindhouse joint projected across an IMAX screen.

"The way I produce now is I produce more like a musician," RZA told UK radio DJ Tim Westwood ahead of *8 Diagrams'* release. "In the old days, I produced more like a DJ. I didn't understand music theory at all. Now that I do understand music theory, I make my music more playable, meaning not only could you listen to it, you could get someone else to play it. Before, you couldn't even write down Wu-Tang music."

Opener "Campfire" plays like the kind of mysticism best absorbed around an open air flame. Dense dialogue from the 1976 movie *Writing Kung Fu* takes up a huge amount of space. "Today, I'll talk about kindness. Justice, faith, and kindness. I want you to listen carefully," says the wise old master, doubling as RZA's voice. The sampled Persuasion's cover of Curtis Mayfield's "Gypsy Woman" sounds like the doomed hum of soldiers marching off to an already lost battle. Clocks tick, gunshots ring out. The drums come down hard, the twisted strings add traditional Wu atmospherics. It's one of the all-time great dramatic openers. "On anything that RZA throw, Ironman's invisible," spits Ghostface Killah. A statement that, in hindsight, reveals a conflict that was brewing.

In contrast, "Rushing Elephants" stomps as hard as anything in the Wu canon. If "Campfire" charts the march of the soldiers, then this is the summoning of the heavy artillery. It's the kind of beat only RZA could serve up, with the level of thump that would have most rappers thinking about slowly walking towards the studio door and running down the street from this mad man. Instead, GZA ponders the Clan's collective strength: "It was not a hobby, but a childhood passion/That had started in the lobby and was quickly fashioned/Every line to line, bar for bar is clockwork/Hazardous and powerful enough to have your block hurt."

Old-fashioned Wu storytelling is there, too. "Get Them Out Ya Way Pa" shuffles and moves like stick-up men creeping on their next victim before exploding into a sprint. The tag-team chorus yells of Ghost and Raekwon sound like two old muggers clearing a path as they run for home. The bass is turned way up, electric guitar squiggles wrap themselves around the mix. It's a low-key beat, but effective. Elsewhere, "Stick Me For My Riches" plays like a Blaxploitation flick, with the Manhattans' Gerald Alston, a 1970s survivor, in the lead role. "I'm searching everyday to find a better way, I've gotta/Hustle still to get my pay before I hit bottom," the weathered singer croons. The track's shimmering cinematics might be the closest musical connection to RZA's soon to be fully realised interest in filmmaking.

The cinematics keep coming. The horror-movie strings of "Unpredictable" and the Spaghetti Western murmurs on "Wolves" play alongside the more traditional Wu monastery meditations of

"Gun Will Go" and "Weak Spot." Lyrically, the group deliver time-honoured Clan takes, spitting shady street chronicles draped with pop culture references. All that's missing is the sound and fury of Ol' Dirty Bastard, three years gone and memorialised in the heartfelt "Life Changes."

As a rapper, RZA also experiments with new flourishes in his style. "Sunlight," in particular, sees him sink into a more spoken word form. He sounds like a wandering soul, drifting the ancient Chinese landscapes that exist in the kung fu universes he so cherishes. He uses Supreme Mathematics to map out the landscape, and calls out to Allah multiple times to give guidance in traversing it ("Allah's the father of all, why do you doubt him?"). This was gunpowder in the musket. RZA's sword sharpened to cut diamond. The musings of a deep thinker, comfortable with the pen and fearless on the mic.

8 Diagrams dropped at a time when New York hip-hop was at its absolute lowest point. The power and ingenuity had shifted to the South, where the traditionally insular scene was simultaneously putting out the hottest singles and harnessing the internet better than any other region. The popularity of crunk had dissolved. In its place, T.I.'s star was on the rise. Clipse's coke rap seeped up the nostrils with more acidic burn than any other music on the planet. Lil Wayne declared himself the best rapper alive and nobody on the East Coast seemed to complain. Nas bemoaned rap's demise by releasing *Hip-Hop is Dead* and few wanted to clap back.

But "how could hip-hop be dead if Wu-Tang is forever?" retorted RZA in a statement. *8 Diagrams* was the chief indicator. Out-of-step with almost every other album of its day, this was music made for grown ups—rap at its broadest, driven by an artist with no creative ceiling.

SO WHY DID GHOSTFACE KILLAH HATE THE ALBUM?

raekwon, Method Man and Ghost's post-*8 Diagrams* rebellion represented the most potentially corrosive inter-Clan beef since the group's foundation and the zenith of tension between Ghost and RZA. The trio didn't like the record, that much is clear, but unpacking the issue points to far more going on under the surface than stylistic disagreements.

The fracturing of the Wu is a well-worn tale—it starts when the money isn't right. The almighty dollar can slither into the smallest cracks and drive wedges between the tightest allies. In the case of Dennis Coles and Robert Diggs, things came to a head in 2005, when the former sued for unpaid royalties and the latter claimed that his 50 percent take was standard. Ghost would prevail shortly before *8 Diagrams*' release. His reaction was more jubilant than maybe it ought to have been: "I just won my court case from them n***as. The suit been in there for three years. So put that out there. They just lost their fuckin' case. So who don't owe who money? Let's get it straight, RZA. That's all I'm sayin', baby. It was a loss, they lost. L-O-S-T. That's really it."

It's sad when families can't resolve their differences outside of a court of law. It's like an acknowledgement that there is a gulf that can never be bridged—not even by shared DNA. Ghost and RZA weren't blood, but shared a bond akin to the disciplined, incorruptible Shaolin monks who they so likened themselves to. But money meant nothing in the forests of Shaoshi mountain. In modern day America, it's emperor, shogun, and king. That shit got to the point it did with Ghostface and RZA was more than a warning. It could easily have been a sorry end to the duo's shared journey.

But the dispute seemed to be only temporary. In an interview with MTV Base ahead of 8 *Diagrams*, RZA seemed not overly concerned when alluding to beef among Clan members: "Over the years, some of us have grown in doubt, or maybe some of us have grown creatively in different directions," he said. "But I will say that when we do come together, a lot of things just seem to evaporate. When we get on the stage together, we can have a problem 10 minutes before we get onstage. But once we're onstage, we feel like everything evaporates."

Ghost wasn't the first member to rebel against the Abbott's leadership. As early as 1997, RZA had been left frustrated by the Clan's lack of enthusiasm to tour with Rage Against the Machine, seeing it as a missed opportunity to both line their pockets and build their rep. Rumours surrounded the release of the 2001 record *Iron Flag* that all was not well within the Wu ("Internal bullshit," Method Man called it). In 2004, U-God officially left the group for a short period, accusing RZA of being the devil and a slavemaster, and of favoring certain members' projects over his. In 2016, U-God filed a lawsuit against RZA and Mitchell "Divine" Diggs, RZA's brother and a key figure in the Wu enterprise, calling out their abuse of power and claiming unpaid royalties.

Ghost, Rae, and Meth claimed their issues with *8 Diagrams* centered on its shift away from the hardened street sound they considered a core tenet of the Clan's ethos. They wanted back into the 36th Chamber, as though Wu-Tang Forever meant calcifying their sound and remaining static until the end of time. The inherent Wu-ness of their subsequent solo output—Raekwon's in particular—indicate that their claims were genuine, but whatever the reason, this lack of trust does seem to hinder the final product. Ghost makes fleeting appearances on *8 Diagrams*' first half and disappears completely over the album's second. Inexplicably, he's the only original member not on the ODB tribute "Life Changes." And yet, he still serves up some of the album's most memorable moments.

Starks had been sweet on George Harrison's beloved Beatles axe workout "While My Guitar Gently Weeps" for a while. He'd already sampled the song on "Black Cream" (sometimes posted online as "Guitar," or "My Guitar"), which hit the sizeable pile of five-star *Pretty Toney Album* lost cuts, most likely—as was the case with a lot of joints during Ghost's middle era—because of problems clearing the sample. Rescued for the *Hidden Darts* compilation, the song is the rapper at peak-level. Over a swarm of electric guitar fiddles and a gently caressed organ, Ghost low-key channels the original's melody in his rhyming before breaking out into full chanting on the hook. He sounds loose, like he went into the booth with memories on his mind of stepping to a snitch and just laid it all out with little thought or effort. It takes a special kind of genius to be this good while sounding so off-the-cuff.

On *8 Diagrams'* "The Heart Gently Weeps," RZA's production adds extra musicality. Ghost's original two-and-a-half-minute running time is expanded to over five-and-a-half epic minutes, the spirit of the original kept alive through guitar lines from Red Hot Chili Peppers' John Frusciante, and Dhani Harrison, George Harrison's son. The ever-sultry Erykah Badu gives a soulful take on the original "While My Guitar Gently Weeps" vocal, and Raekwon and Meth perform their verses admirably, but it's Ghostface Killah who comes in like a double-barreled shotgun blast.

Telling the tale of being stepped to in a supermarket by the nephew of one of his victims, Ghost builds a sweeping narrative through minutiae: warm blood and cold steel, angry mothers and crying babies, dry mouths and wet Wallabees. "First thought was to snatch the ratchet/Said fuck it and fuckin' grabbed it/I ducked, he bucked twice, this n***a was fuckin' laughin'/I wrestled him to the ground, tustle, scuffle, constantly kicked him."

This was expert storytelling, with Ghost playing the De Niro to RZA's Scorsese. "The Heart Gently Weeps" is Exhibit A of what an in-tune pair could do. What was bubbling under the surface is impossible to detect.

JUST HOW MUCH OF GHOST'S DISSENT WAS CENTERED IN A disagreement on the album's sound and how much was down to lingering issues outside the booth? Or maybe Dennis Coles—one of the best artists on the planet at the end of 2007—was just done with being told what to do.

In November 2007, Ghostface told *Rap Basement*: "[RZA] wanted to make [*8 Diagrams*] how he wanted it and it ain't come out right. He wanna always do the whole thing himself, produce the whole album. We're like, let's bring in some other producers too. Bring in Kanye, bring in Pharrell. You ain't gotta do the whole thing yourself. He wanna make his own instruments and shit and it sounded real horrible."

I get it. How could an artist making some of the greatest music the earth has ever seen feel comfortable with just one hand on the wheel? It's natural when you're operating on such a high level to be resistant to anyone else calling the shots. RZA knew it to be true. It's why he always envisioned the Wu transforming from a dictatorship to a democracy. The timeline of his five-year master plan was no accident. He was the Abbott, not the shogun. He couldn't rule over eight artists with an iron fist forever.

In a move that rang with bold defiance, Ghost released *The Big Doe Rehab* just one week before *8 Diagrams*, having previously touted the possibility of dropping it on the same day. The record proved a perfect microcosm of RZA-free Ghost as an artist—the breezy soul samples, rich narratives he'd perfected outside his mentor's gaze, and memorable hooks, all present. Then came the rumours of a Wu-Tang album in the pipeline without RZA's involvement. The provocative *Shaolin vs Wu-Tang* title was eventually stamped onto Raekwon's solid 2011 record. When asked about the album in an interview with *Entertainment Weekly*, his answer was revealing.

"It's not nothing derogatory towards Wu. It's just that Shaolin is the place, Wu-Tang is the crew that came from that place. It's like me just going back to my history of being an emcee first, before I actually became part of Wu-Tang."

Rae continued, "I always give RZA that support as far as saying he brought Wu-Tang to the table. It was his philosophy. He picked certain dudes to be part of this group, and he said, 'This is what it's going to be called.' Before that, I was on the block. I was living in Shaolin. So this album just shows the street side of me, challenging the great side of Wu-Tang. Which is almost like how T.I. did *T.I. vs. T.I.P.* You're going to get sounds that relate to Wu-Tang. You're going to get sounds that relate to great Rae at his best shit, too. You're going to get a lot of animation as far as the skits are concerned. It's going to be a hot one. Everyone's going to love it."

But if the album is the pre-RZA prequel, why does every producer tug at RZA's style? Scram Jones, Bronze Nazareth, Oh No, etc., all worshipped at the gates of the temple of the 36 Chambers. *Shaolin vs Wu-Tang* underlined that the Wu will always be one—that the spiritual connection can't easily be broken by petty squabbles or courtroom drama.

A follow-up to *8 Diagrams* would have to wait seven years. Released in 2014, *A Better Tomorrow* brought back the snappy hip-hop breaks but, as far as being a late-career surge of inspiration, this was no *Abbey Road*. The group dynamic sounded tired, the album badly missed the Clan's magic.

And so *8 Diagrams* might be the last great Wu-Tang group record and it plays as such. Like one of those great final-day band albums, it reflects the chaos it was born into. It's untamed and unrefined, but it's extraordinary.

MODERN BEEFS AND THE CAPITALIST CRUSH

"King of the jungle, ain't shit about me humble."

IN THIS VERY MODERN BEEF, GHOSTFACE KILLAH FIRED THE heavy artillery through the portal of YouTube. No beat was paid for, no microphone necessary. Action Bronson was reprimanded for his crimes in absentia.

In this war, Marcellus Wiley and Max Kellerman filled in for Gavrilo Princip. It was 2015 and, due to some surface-level vocal similarities, an emerging Bronsolini had endured one million Ghostface comparisons. When probed in an interview by *SportsNation* hosts Wiley and Kellerman on the similarities, a frustrated Bronson paid some respect ("I'm just glad it's one of the greats") before dropping an ill-advised sound bite: "[Ghostface] isn't rapping like this no more." A miniature Bill Duke from *Menace II* Society probably rattled around his head in the immediate aftermath. "You know you done fucked up, don't you?"

Ghost's reply was part-comedy, part-pageantry. "You've got this little fake ass n***a, Action Bronson, running around sounding like me," he sneers to a cellphone camera in the six-and-a-half-minute response video. "But I want to tell this little fat fuck something: I gave you a grace period, n***a. I was supposed to destroy you a long time ago. You go on *SportsNation*, kicking that shit, acting like, yo, you the n***a... First of all, you little fat fuck, who gives you the right to even mention my name out your motherfucking mouth? Boy, you done made a mistake."

Never mind that, just months earlier, Ghostface had admitted to *VladTV* that he'd previously mistaken Bronson's voice for his own. ("I'm asking myself, 'When the fuck I do that verse?'" he said amusingly). Leave it to Tony Starks to threaten to set his enemy's beard on fire while Teddy Pendergrass's "Be for Real" plays in the background.

What Ghost didn't do, of course, was respond with a verse, which would have been appropriate given Bronson questioned the veracity of his flow. But it didn't matter. Bronson was wise enough to not enter a war of words with one of his true stylistic forefathers and soon ceded the victory. That was that. Nobody had the appetite to see these two guys butt heads.

Ghost's cultural impact had begun to dwindle as the 2010s lurched on and the quality of his records began to fade. Yet fate had seemingly demanded that he be embroiled in two very modern beefs. First, this mild slapping down of Action Bronson. Then, the more sinister dealings with the CEO of Turing Pharmaceuticals, Martin Shkreli. These were disputes that undeniably seemed silly on a surface level, yet tell us a lot about a new age of rap warfare.

Capitalism has been a key ripple in hip-hop since the first songs graduated from Bronx parties to vinyl pressings. There are not too many rappers preaching socialist, Marxist thinking. Trust me, I've looked for them. Sean "Puffy" Combs pouring his own brand of alcoholic beverages is lionized as entrepreneurial genius. Jay-Z has subscribed to an idea first presented by Justin Timberlake's depiction of Shaun Parker in *The Social Network*: "A million dollars isn't cool. You know what's cool? A billion dollars."

Billionaires should not exist. Still, Dame Dash wasn't wrong when he told Bill O'Reilly that, "If an 11-year-old were to imitate Cam'ron, they would become the CEO of their own company. They would control their own destiny, and take a bad situation and make it good." But the true face of degenerative American capitalism is a douchey "pharma bro" who, thanks to a few breaks in life, found himself in a position where he could jack up the price of the antiparasitic drug Daraprim, commonly used by AIDS patients, from $13.50 to $750. Per pill. Bernie Sanders called Shkreli the "poster child of greed."

After the 2015 Daraprim story broke and his profile shot up overnight, Shkreli was unrepentant about his business strategy, pointing out the factors that dictate drug economy in the US. And he wasn't wrong. Any society that commodifies human health and makes business out of life and death deserves to take plenty of the flack.

In any case, Shkreli was happy to play the villain. It was a role he took up with ease. (He even seems happy to present himself as nefarious, like the kind of kid Dr. Evil thought his frozen semen had created before Seth Green showed up.)

Next thing you know, he's flaunting his wealth by purchasing a lavish Wu-Tang Clan art piece.

How odd that the Clan unintentionally inserted themselves into this sorry story of American excess. Yet the moment RZA declared that their new double album *Once Upon a Time in Shaolin* would be released as a single copy encased in a high-security silver box, available to one buyer through an auction, the wheels of fate seemed certain to be taking the group towards disaster.

The story goes that the project was willed into existence not by RZA, but by Tarik Azzougarh, aka Cilvaringz, a Dutch rapper-producer who became a Clan affiliate after jumping on-stage with the group during a concert in Amsterdam back in 1997. Under RZA's watch, much of Cilvaringz' early work went into his debut album *I*, which dropped belatedly in 2007. It's an alright record. Cilvaringz is a below-par rapper and looked to guests to help with the heavy lifting (Ghost shows up with Raekwon and RZA on "Weeping Tiger"). About half the production on *I* is handled by Cilvaringz too, with his mentor clocking up a handful of credits and the rest taken care of by various other beatmakers in the Wu universe—Bronze Nazareth, 4th Disciple, Mathematics, True Master, Moongod Allah. It's a suite that revels in the original tenets of the Wu's sonic philosophy—rich, rugged, and hard-hitting—while lacking that extra 10 percent of intangible genius you feel in their best releases.

From there, Cilvaringz began work on an open-ended project that neither he nor RZA went into with a clear goal in mind. But, as detailed in Cyrus Bozorgmehr's book, also titled *Once Upon a Time in Shaolin*, the sessions began to yield results that Cilvaringz believed sounded like a Wu-Tang Clan album. (Bozorgmehr served as a senior advisor after it was decided to turn the album into a high-end art piece.)

For six years Cilvaringz helmed the recording sessions, which mostly took place in the picturesque panorama of Marrakech, Morocco. You'll sometimes see the word "secret" used to describe the sessions, which is probably an exaggeration. For sure, though, there was no hype around this music, no anticipation that a classic group album was in the pipeline. In fact, various Clan members have claimed they had no real knowledge of what the sessions were supposed to add up to. And so the opportunity was there to do a little something different with the project. The decision was made—as a push back to modern day piracy and streaming, which RZA and Cilvaringz felt had cheapened music as an art form, only one copy of *Once Upon a Time in Shaolin* would be produced and sold to the highest bidder.

Really, who did they expect to buy this thing? Someone doing it for the culture? Only villains lay out such extravagant amounts on exclusive pieces that can be described as high-end. In 2018, Banksy attempted to send up the ridiculousness of art as a commodity by shredding a painting right after it had been sold for £1.04 million. Yet as soon as the act was completed, he'd created a whole new monster. Sotheby's released a statement that said, "Banksy didn't destroy an artwork in the auction, he created one." Art can be a self-sustaining beast.

With the collapse of album sales, a lot of alternative thinking has gone into finding ways of making music a profitable pursuit. Mach-Hommy's erratic pricing policy has seen him sell albums for such random figures as $111.11, $187, $300, all the way up to $1,000. I used to think this was nuts. That is, until another independent rapper pointed out to me that Hommy can rake in more money selling one album than most artists can make selling a stack of downloads on Bandcamp for $5 or $10 a piece. For a rapper probably working paycheck to paycheck to keep music as his full-time profession, you can't be mad at Hommy for finding an economic blueprint that works.

Still, *Once Upon a Time in Shaolin* makes me deeply uncomfortable. This was the worst tactic the Wu could have pursued. It's art for elites—Shkreli is reported to have paid $2 million for this thing. It puts music out of reach of the masses and into the hands of those with the least noble intentions. You can picture a hip-hop version of *Jurassic Park*'s sleazy lawyer Donald Gennaro in the background. When's our coupon day? Do we ever get to hear this record?

Our music collections say so much about us. Each record

carefully sitting on your shelf is a little component of your personality. You can tell a lot about a person by how many Lil Wayne songs sit in their iTunes library. What our music collections shouldn't tell is our economic status. I'm reminded of Paul Ashworth, the disheveled Arsenal fan from the British movie *Fever Pitch*. Asked if he'd be interested in applying for a better job in the school he works at, Ashworth declines with an assertion that extra money means little to him: "Well, I've got enough to pay my rent, I got enough for my season ticket and a couple of records a month." You can't take music away and siphon it off for those fortunate enough to be making extra scratch.

The paradox is that simply by talking about the album's distribution and the wider issue of music as a money-making pursuit, I've affirmed its artistic value. It's a shame that the conversations RZA and Cilvaringz hoped to stimulate were drowned out by the voice of the wicked figure the press loved to call "the most hated man in America."

In truth, *Once Upon a Time in Shaolin* is probably more fun to talk about than it is to listen to. A certain amount of myth-making sprouted up around the record. What are we to imagine when guest vocalists include *Game of Thrones*' Carice van Houton, Cher, and members of the FC Barcelona squad? The best story was an alleged (and fake) special clause stating that the Wu-Tang Clan or Bill Murray could make an attempt to break into the purchaser's home and steal it back at any point in the future.

There was an amusing ripple to the story in 2017, when *Harper's* posted transcripts of jury selection from a trial that saw Shkreli convicted of three counts of fraud in a Manhattan federal court. A lot of potential jurors were happy to express their extreme distaste for Shkreli ("The only thing I'd be impartial about is what prison this guy goes to"), but the most hilarious were those who showed their loyalty to the Clan. Here's a sample:

> **JUROR NO 59**: "Your Honor, totally he is guilty and in no way can I let him slide out of anything because..."
> **THE COURT**: "OK. Is that your attitude toward anyone charged with a crime who has not been proven guilty?"
> **JUROR NO 59**: "It's my attitude toward his entire demeanor, what he has done to people."
> **THE COURT**: "All right. We are going to excuse you, sir."
> **JUROR NO 59**: "And he disrespected the Wu-Tang Clan."

Before Shkreli faced the criminal justice system, he attempted to stare down Ghostface Killah. It was January 2016 and Shkreli had already been arrested on charges of securities fraud. After it was revealed that one of America's most despised individuals owned *Once Upon a Time in Shaolin*, it was Ghost who appointed himself official spokesman for the Wu-Tang Clan, calling the businessman a "shithead" and attacking his decision to raise the price of Daraprim. "I don't even know him," Ghost told *TMZ*. "But I know what he did with the AIDS [drug]—like that, that's not right, that's not right." Shkreli responded to Ghostface on Twitter, calling him a "non-profit rapper," at which point Ghost took it back to *TMZ*, telling his opponent: "I'll break your heart in four days."

Shkreli, forever reveling in his own puffed-up villainy, dropped a "dis video" in which he and masked goons threatened to erase Starks' verses from *Once Upon a Time in Shaolin*. "You're an old man—you're an old man that's lost his relevance, and you're trying to reclaim the spotlight from my spotlight," says Shkreli, sipping on a glass of red wine.

Ghost fired back with his own dis video, comparing Shkreli's physicality to Peter Pan ("the man with the 12-year-old body") and criticizing his decision to ratchet up the price of Daraprim by calling him a "real killer, a soft killer... you're a baby." Ghost even calls on the support of his mom and sister. It's two men trying to out-ridiculous one another. That is, until Ghostface's sister emotionally recounts needing brain surgery without being blessed with insurance.

What did all this silliness achieve? These were beefs for spectacle, not supremacy. Beefs to start Twitter conversation, beefs to fuel memes. In this modern climate, even when bars are spit, the big weapons are no longer words recited in a booth. We saw it in the high profile bout between Drake and Meek Mill. The dis tracks on both sides were clearly weak, but Drake instinctively knew how the internet works. At the 2015 OVO Festival in Toronto, during the height of the feud, he performed with various anti-Meek memes flashing behind him on a big screen, a sad indicator of what he viewed as defining winners and losers. It took Pusha T's evisceration of Drizzy in 2018 to roll back the years. A good old-fashioned example of words as bullets. Faced with that kind of onslaught, Drake had no answer.

Is a rap beef truly a rap beef if no bars are spit? Ghost's battles with Bronson and Shkreli were closer to his comic book forays. He'd tackled fake enemies on *36 Seasons*; the natural extension was to take down a rapper with the build of the Kingpin, and a businessman who probably fancied himself as a Norman Osborn.

So why does Ghost do it? Probably because he's a comedian. It's an element of his persona that hasn't been dimmed even as his musical output has slipped from the dizzying heights it once enjoyed.

His legacy long secure, it doesn't really matter if Ghost indulges in some antics for his own amusement. Why be famous if you can't get a kick out of it? Ghost finds himself in hilarious narratives that undeniably amuse me. But I can't help but feel that the lack of actual rapping in these rap beefs was somewhat damning for the form. Tony Starks passed up the opportunity to strap on his metal suit, particularly disappointing when he had an opponent like Shkreli—the epitome of a very modern, very American, evil—in his sights. Go all in for all that is good.

WAKE THE TOWN AND TELL THE PEOPLE

"They wrote our name in the sky, see baby, we 'bout it!"

TRY TO PICTURE THIS UNREMARKABLE SCENE. IT WAS 2017, that soul-chilling, spirit-corroding year of so much demonry, and I was sipping beer in the Duke of Sussex, the small pub in Peckham, South London—deep in the heart of grime country— that I called my local haunt at the time. It was Thursday quiz night, I think, but my memory might be letting me down here.

Drinking in a nearby bar isn't like, say, going to gigs, when every experience should be different and the memories distinct. The best live shows become bookmarks over the course of a life. When a band or artist steps on stage, their ultimate motivation should be to make you say, "I was there," but we drink in local pubs partly for the feeling of familiarity. The comfortable, informal atmosphere brought about by the same faces ordering the same drinks and glaring at the same TV screens. That's why on this indistinguishable night I was perched at the section of the bar where I always sat. Among the blurry memories (the alcohol threw an extra layer of haze on top), I do remember Dawn Penn's "You Don't Love Me (No, No, No)" coming through the speakers.

My head instantly lifted a few inches as the slick tune slithered down my ear canal. What a number! A rocksteady jam that slinks and bops with a poised cool-as-hellness. The track has a distinct opening too, with an anonymous male voice shouting an ultimate rallying call: "Wa-wa-wa-wake the town and tell the people, 'bout the musical disc coming your way!" From there you get some rapid-fire orchestral stabs as that same voice continues the call to the floor with hype-man shouts of "Buh-buh-buh-bow!" Then there's a drum roll and, just before Penn's groovy vocals kick in, I remember shouting over my beer, "GHOST! FACE! KILLAAAHHHH!"

That's because my relationship with the original is too entangled with "No No No," the Ghostface tune that sees the rapper announce himself with the kind of gusto I tried to replicate in the Duke of Sussex. Forget chop-up-the-soul sampling. On "No No No," which appears on rarities compilation *Hidden Darts* (I suspect it was deleted from *The Pretty Toney Album*'s tracklisting because of sample issues), Ghost spits over the entire song unaltered—vocals and all.

"I'd love to make you happy, buy an island off Miami," Ghost raps silkily. Underneath, Penn's sun-saturated vocals float and bounce gorgeously. Ghost even flips the track into a duet at one point, replying to Penn's croons of, "You left me," with the retort, "I never left you, you left me." The audacity of him to dispute Penn. The gall of this man to expect listeners to put up with him trampling on "You Don't Love Me (No, No, No)"—a perfect, unimpeachable piece of art. And yet, it works. The track is pure confidence from Ghost. A spectacular piece of artistic appropriation you can't help but be dazzled by.

He's repeated the trick on tracks like "Holla." Spitting over

1970s soul mavens The Delfonics and their sweet joint "La-La Means I Love You," Ghost hilariously transforms the syrupy chorus into melodic shouts of, "Holla, holla, holla if you want to/I'll bust you!" And, incredibly, on "ABC," Ghost jacks the Jackson 5's ubiquitous classic and manages to make the exercise worthwhile.

In almost every known instance of him rapping over classic cuts wholesale, Ghost stays silent for a period, giving the original significant time to ride on its own. I don't know if this is a respect thing, as though he feels he just has to pass the mic to these legends. Or maybe he's just doing it as a fan—he's paid for these samples (sometimes), and he's going to showcase as many of those classic vibes on his records as possible. What's undeniable is that Dennis Coles is a music lover. When I saw him perform in Dublin in 2017, he even took a few minutes just to vibe out to an Al Green record.

Ghost is one of the greatest emcees to ever rap on soul samples. As tense and tightly wound as the production on *Supreme Clientele* felt, it was built around finely carved '70s loops. J Dilla's *Donuts* were cuts the beatmaker figured were impossible for rappers to harness, yet Ghost managed to rein a couple in on "Whip You With a Strap" and "Beauty Jackson." He loved soul so much, he conceived the idea for *Ghostdini: Wizard of Poetry in Emerald City*, a collection of love joints that sees Ghost mostly spit over heartfelt R&B grooves (with him adorably asking his girl to rub his belly on "Baby") and his classic chopped-up-soul numbers (over the mean 1970s-style grooves of narrative-driven number "Guest House," Ghost plays a wronged husband in a soap opera-esque tale of infidelity). *Ghostdini* isn't in Ghost's canon of five-star albums, but it's a decent gem in the catalogue—the concept alone reveals the soulful side to his spirit.

THE ART OF UNEARTHING A PIECE OF CAKED-IN-DUST, analogue audio and transforming it into something new, singular, and supreme is as important a factor in hip-hop history as the two turntables and a microphone. Through his heightened affinity for old soul samples, Ghostface Killah, a maverick in the tradition of the Dadaist movement, challenged established canons of art, thought, and morality. He's a rap game Raoul Hausmann, piecing together shards of old 7-inch soul in much the same way as the German blazed the unconventional style of art known as photomontage. He's Andy Warhol, taking "You Don't Love Me (No, No, No)" and recontextualizing it in the same way the pop artist once jacked the Campbell's soup can.

Or maybe he's Richard Prince, the infamous appropriation artist who "rephotographed" images originally shot for Marlboro ad campaigns, cropping out all text and logos. In doing so, Prince presented clichés of advertising and mass media in a gallery space—traditionally a no-go zone for editorial or commercial photography—forcing his audience to confront how these messages and iconography are nothing but fiction.

More recently, Prince put together a series of framed Instagram snaps, his only addition to other people's images were the oddball comments he made beneath the photographs themselves. The pieces sold for as much as $100,000, with not a penny going to the person who captured the image on their smartphone. "Trolling" is how a bunch of news outlets put it but, like his best work, Prince tests the boundaries of copyright law and challenges the meaning of ownership. He's spent his whole career battling lawsuits.

As Sam Abell said to *Time*, "As a photographer on the Marlboro campaign, one of the things that bothers me about Prince's appropriation is that it's without risk for him. He's taken failure out of the artistic equation." Ghost takes old cuts, sheds them of absolutely nothing and yet creates new art. Like Prince's detractors, there are those who will consider it nothing more than a jack move. Sampling isn't to everyone's taste. When Kanye West looped Daft Punk's "Harder, Better, Faster, Stronger" into his own synth-heavy, neon-lit glamorama "Stronger" and ran all the way to mainstream radio, I remember the horror among some. Freda Payne once told me of her disappointment that her song "I Get High (On Your Memory)" had been flipped into a weed anthem, presumably referring to Styles P's "High."

Controversy is a necessary friction. Andy Warhol, Richard Prince, Dennis Coles—three great American artists, no two of whom are exactly alike, but all of whom challenge the ideas of ownership. At its most basic level, Prince's work sparks debate about the concept of copyright. Whatever you think of his techniques, the very presence of that debate makes his work art.

Ghost does what he does, I suspect, because he loves to groove to old tunes. I don't know whether his foray into rapping over live bands on the *Twelve Reasons to Die* records, *36 Seasons,* and *Sour Soul* represented a total change-up in ethos or if it was just the natural evolution. Either way, it underlined his affinity to the old school—no throwback Instagram filters necessary.

Ghostface Killah was only in his mid-20s when he first emerged but he never seemed that young. The raw, smoky gruffness of his vocal cords has always sounded like they've been doused in hours of soul and filtered through too many blunts. The venom that emanates lacks any youthful exuberance. Call him an old soul if you want to be trite, but no doubt he's always drawn heavily from his stylistic forefathers.

But no comparisons to high art or cultural analysis matter when the drums kick in on "No No No" and Ghost's flow is in full-flight. Dawn Penn's jam has become a pop culture staple, covered by Rihanna, performed live by Beyoncé, and strongly worked into Lily Allen's "Shame for You" without accreditation. But Ghost's version is my favorite, the one that best honors Penn's swaggering style. Her classic track can be heard intact, but "No No No" is still as fresh as a day-old dye job.

Afterword

A LETTER FROM STATEN ISLAND

"You can look me dead in my eyes, I was made for this."

FROM BROOKLYN, I JUMPED THE J TRAIN AND HEADED towards Lower Manhattan. Final destination? Staten Island. Shaolin. 58.5 square miles of sprawling New York land. Home of the Wu-Tang Clan. For me, this would be a pilgrimage as important as the Catholic's journey to Medjugorje; the Muslim's to Mecca. We are, after all, talking about sacred land destined to be mapped and documented in the holy book of hip-hop.

Gotham is studded with rap landmarks. I've visited the front steps where The Notorious B.I.G. sat as a child, frozen as other kids skipped past, his mother Voletta Wallace maintaining her stare at the back of her son's head. I've walked the same uptown streets as Big L and Cam'ron. But I'd never laid eyes on the land of the Wu. Seemed like a pretty significant thing to do as part of my research for a book on Ghostface Killah, though I'd no real plan for the trip other than taking a glance at the building he grew up in. Sharing the same space as someone of historic importance is why I imagine people still flock to Tombstone and the scene of the Gunfight at the OK Corral, even if nobody has ever seen Wyatt Earp rock a mic on-stage.

The very fact that the ferry is the handiest mode of transport here highlights the cut-off nature of the island. That this huge part of a modern city requires such a very old-fashioned lifeline is quite surreal. The ferry terminal felt like a bus or train station, better suited for long-distance journeys than a couple-mile jaunt over some water. I sauntered aboard, though, and, despite the winter conditions, took a place outside the protection of the ferry walls so I could enjoy the view.

It was bitterly cold on the water, but I tactically stood right in front of an open door that led into the heated ferry. Every few seconds, a wave of warm air emanating from the door would wash over me, keeping away the chill. I stared at the Statue of Liberty while simultaneously trying to stay out of photographs tourists were taking. One person copied the pose of the Mother of Exiles, arm in the air. I've been out to the statue and to Ellis Island a couple of times, but had never made this 25-mile trek out to Staten Island. In fact, neither had the friend I met for beer just a couple of nights ago, despite being a life-long New Yorker. 'The forgotten borough,' they call it. I get that vibe.

The ferry safely docked and the passengers disembarked. Those who had made the trip 1,000 times before were first, I imagine. Locals probably perch themselves near the doors and swiftly find dry land as us sightseers slowly snake our way down the narrow stairs.

My plan was to walk from the Staten Island Ferry terminal to Stapleton Houses, the near-60-year-old housing project that Ghostface Killah once called his home. ("Staple-Land's where the ambulance don't come.") But the island is a sprawling suburbia, each street slightly crooked, almost impossible to navigate when your phone doesn't operate on the New York grid without expensive roaming charges. So, somewhat lost, I scrunched up against the library wall to jack some of their free wifi, put out a beacon for an Uber, and let a metal chariot be my guide.

Calling this trip research is generous to my journalistic integrity. Really, I just wanted to see Stapleton Houses. I can't explain that any more than I can explain why, of all the seeds of ideas I have had, I chose to turn this one into a book. I felt a gravitational pull. I'm sad it took me this long to get to the island.

Why am I writing this book? This is surely an unusual thing for a kid from Ireland to be doing. I had a lot of thoughts about Dennis Coles, that's true. The real answer, though, is as elusive to me as ever. The simplest truth might just be that he is my favorite artist to ever do it.

His legacy is unimpeachable. Even today, years beyond what any fan would reasonably describe as his peak, there are flashes of his genius. Consider the opening lines from his guest spot on Wiki's 2017 track "Made for This," one of his best verses in years: "I was made for this, my bones is titanium/Thoughts that marinate I swear through the cranium." I ask you, who else can write like this? Ghost has always been about swagger and style, but on a deeper level there's that sense of culture and community that cuts through the razor wire world the Wu created on wax. This island is the cradle.

These weren't thoughts I was having in the back of that Uber. I was focused on timekeeping, focused on map checking, focused on completing this strange odyssey. Then it just appeared. Stapleton Houses. Among the relatively anonymous looking homes and businesses surrounding it, the building stood out like a snowball on scorched earth. This was like stumbling upon a military base in the middle of suburbia. Or finding Area 51 on the Las Vegas strip. If you don't believe that America's poor are siphoned off into cage-like dwellings to mentally prepare them for a life in prison, this might offer a convincing argument.

Stapleton Houses are the largest housing development on Staten Island. Ghostface Killah grew up there (Building 218, to be exact) and has never been shy to share that fact in his music.

Only a few months before this trip, some six miles north of where I was living in Peckham, the Grenfell Tower burned. If ever there was a monument to the capitalistic crush poor people find themselves trapped in, it's that charred building. Here's another symbol, but still standing. Temples to the capitalist regime.

I took a few snaps of the building, probably to the bemusement of a driver more used to chauffeuring visitors to the galaxy of typical New York tourist spots. I probed him on the way back to the ferry about whether or not he knew who the Wu-Tang Clan are, but he was more of a classical music guy.

I jumped the ferry back. It amused me that the service was free—a fact that seemed to fly in the face of the American capitalist dream. What of all those taxpayers who'll never use the service? I had to throw my head back and laugh at those poor saps as Wall Street loomed in the distance.

And that was it. I'd seen the ground that functions as this book's origin point, where the seeds were sown and bars were written. I have no idea if, during my brief time on the island, I was sharing the ground with Ghostface Killah. Who knows what Tony Starks is doing at any given time? The possibilities seem infinite when the scope of the universe he created in music eclipses the actual planet we live on. He makes rapping seem so easy, yet so limitless.

BIBLIOGRAPHY

Books

Bozorgmehr, Cyrus, *Once Upon a Time in Shaolin: The Untold Story of the Wu-Tang Clan's Million-Dollar Secret Album, the Devaluation of Music, and America's New Public Enemy No. 1*, Flatiron Books, 2017

Claremont, Chris and John Byrne, *X-Men: The Dark Phoenix Saga*, Marvel, 1980

Fu, Poshek (editor), *China Forever: The Shaw Brothers and Diasporic Cinema*, University of Illinois Press, 2008

Knight, Michael Muhammad, *The Five Percenters: Islam, Hip-Hop and the Gods of New York*, Oneworld Publications, 2008

RZA with Chris Norris, *The Tao of Wu*, Riverhead/Berkley/Penguin Books USA, 2009

RZA with Chris Norris, *The Wu-Tang Manuel*, Riverhead, 2004

U-God, *Raw: My Journey Into the Wu-Tang*, Picador, 2018

Westhoff, Ben, *Original Gangstas*, Hatchette Books, 2016

Films

The 36th Chamber of Shaolin, Dir. Liu Chia-liang, 1978
Comic Book Superheroes Unmasked, Dir. Stephen Kroopnick, 2003
Crouching Tiger, Hidden Dragon, Dir. Ang Lee, 2000
The Education of Sonny Carson, Dir. Michael Campus, 1974
The Eight Diagram Pole Fighter, Dir. Chia-Liang Liu, 1984
Fever Pitch, Dir. David Evans, 1997

Fist of Fury, Dir. Lo Wei, 1972
Five Fingers of Death, Dir. Jeong Chang-hwa, 1972
Glass, Dir. M. Night Shyamalan, 2019
Iron Man, Dir. Jon Favreau, 2008
John Wick, Dir. Chad Stahelski, 2014
Jurassic Park, Dir. Steven Spielberg, 1993
Kill Bill: Vol. 1, Dir. Quentin Tarantino, 2003
Kill Bill: Vol. 2, Dir. Quentin Tarantino, 2004
King of New York, Dir. Abel Ferrera, 1990
Menace II Society, Dir. Allen & Albert Hughes, 1993
The Mystery of Chess Boxing, Dir. Joseph Kuo, 1979
Shaolin and Wu Tang, Dir. Gordon Liur, 1983
Split, Dir. M. Night Shyamalan, 2016
The Social Network, Dir. David Fincher, 2010
Unbreakable, Dir. M. Night Shyamalan, 2000
With Great Power: The Stan Lee Story, Dir. Terry Dougas and Nikki Frakes, 2010
Wu-Tang Clan: Of Mics and Men, Dir. Sacha Jenkins, 2019

Articles

"The 50 Most NYC Albums Ever," *The Village Voice*, February 18, 2014
Ahmed, Insanul, "Method Man Breaks Down His 25 Most Essential Songs," *Complex*, October 19, 2011
Battan, Carrie, "Ghostface Killah Will Be on VH1's 'Couples Therapy'," *Pitchfork*, November 12, 2013
Bonanno, Jonathan "Gotti," "Last Man Standing," *The Source*, issue 126, March, 2000
Boryga, Andrew, "A Museum Quest Spins On and On," *The New York Times*, September 3, 2010
Breihan, Tom, "Album Of The Week: Ghostface Killah 36 Seasons," *Stereogum*, December 9, 2014
Busby, Mattha, "Woman Who Bought Shredded Banksy Artwork Will Go Through With Purchase," *The Guardian*, October 11, 2018
C, Jeff, "Ghostface Killah Talks Goin' To Africa," Rapdirt.com, January 10, 2000
Cohen, Jonathan, "Wu-Tang Clan Eyeing Summer For Comeback Album," *Billboard*, January 24, 2007
Desta, Yohana, "Drake Trolls Meek Mill With Memes at OVO Fest Because He Can," *Mashable*, August 4, 2015
Di Donato, Jill, "Raised By Rap Royalty, Infinite Coles Is Finding Success On His Own," *Nylon*, March 8, 2017
Diva, Amanda, "Ghostface: Change Gon Come," AllHipHop.com, June 2, 2004
Ducker, Eric, "Ghostface Killah: The Balladeer," *The Fader*, issue 37
"Farrakhan Preaches Responsibility At Hip-Hop Summit," *Billboard*, February 18, 2002
Grant, Ural, "Minister Louis Farrakhan Co-Signs JAY-Z's "4:44" Album & Ice Cube's BIG3 Basketball League," *HipHopDX*, August 3, 2017
Griffin, Junius, "Anti-White Harlem Gang Reported to Number 400 Social Worker Says Its Members Are Trained in Crime and Fighting by Defectors

BIBLIOGRAPHY

From Black Muslims," *The New York Times*, May 6, 1964

Griffin, Junius, "Harlem: The Tension Underneath," *The New York Times*, May 29, 1964

Gross, Jason, "RZA's Edge," *Film Comment*, May-June 2008

Gordon, Jeremy, "Ghostface Killah Says He Has Mistaken Action Bronson's Voice for His Own," *Pitchfork*, May 21, 2015

Gordon, Jeremy, "Ghostface Killah Says 'Shithead' Martin Shkreli Should Release One-of-a-Kind Wu-Tang Album," *Pitchfork*, January 22, 2016

Hicks, Jonathan P., "A New Call for Staten Island to Secede," *The New York Times*, December 17, 2008

Higgins, Carter, "Ghostface Killah: On a Mission To Make Diabetes Ghost," Blackdoctor.org, May 9, 2016"

"History: A Timeline of Staten Island," SILive.com, April 21, 2010

Johnson, Christopher, "God, the Black Man and the Five Percenters," *NPR*, August 4, 2006

Kaur, Harmeet, "New York City Now Has a Wu-Tang Clan District," CNN.com, May 5, 2019

Kimble, Julian, "Which NYC Housing Projects Have Produced the Most Famous People?" *Complex*, September 26, 2013

Kovar, Sweeney, "I Still Got a Story to Tell": Wu-Tang Clans's Ghostface Killah Talks Growing Old, Finding God and Twelve Reasons to Die," *FACT*, April 16, 2013

Knight, Michael Muhammad, "Remembering Master Fard Muhammad," *Vice*, February 28, 2013

LeRoy, Dan, "MF DOOM Biography," Allmusic.com

Lockett, Dee, "U-God Is Suing RZA and Wu-Tang Clan for $2.5 Million Because Some Beefs Are Forever," *Vulture*, November 30, 2016

Ma, David, "The Champ," *Wax Poetics*, issue 61, March, 2015

Martinez, Rafael, "Keep It Movin'," *Prefix*, May 5, 2006

Matteo, Thomas, "Staten Island's Role in the Civil War," SILive.com, September 25, 2011

Mlynar, Phillip, "Q&A: Rapper 9th Prince On His Older Brother RZA And The Early Days Of The Wu-Tang Clan, the *Village Voice*, October 4, 2010

Nelson, Chris, "Jailed Ghostface Killah to Answer Weapon Charge," MTV.com, February 9, 1999

Plaugic, Lizzue, "The story of Richard Prince and his $100,000 Instagram art," *The Verge*, May 30, 2015

Pollock, Andrew, "Drug Goes From $13.50 a Tablet to $750, Overnight," *The New York Times*, September 20, 2015

"Public Enemy," *Harper's*, Septembers 2017

Rabin, Nathan, Interview: Ghostface Killah," *The A.V. Club*, May 17, 2006

Reed, Davy, "Ghostface Killah always has a story to tell," *Crack*

Rosenthal, Jeff, "A Comprehensive History of Wu-Tang Clan's Endless Beefs," *Vulture*, April 24, 2014

Siu, Stephen H. Y., "A New Made in Hong Kong Label," *The Montreal Gazette*, 16 September, 1972

Tardio, Andres, "RZA Opens Up About Wu Tang Problems," HipHopDX.com,

November 29, 2007

Vozick-Levinson, Simon, "Raekwon on Wu-Massacre, the Future of the Wu-Tang Clan, His Label Dreams, and More," *Entertainment Weekly*, February 19, 2010

Wachs, Audrey, "A Torrent of New Projects on Staten Island are Reshaping the Once-Forgotten Borough," *The Architects Newspaper*, June 9, 2016

Wagner, Jason, "Ghostface Not Co-Signing New Wu-Tang CD," *Rap Basement*, November 30, 2007

Ware, Lawrence, "Let's All Remember The Time Bill O'Reilly Got His Ass Handed To Him By Cam'ron," *The Root*, April 27, 2017

"Wu-Tang's Ghostface Killah Arrested on Weapons Charges," MTV.com, December 11, 1997

Young, Alex, "Ghostface Killah Responds to Martin Shkreli: "The Man With the 12-year-old Body," *Consequence of Sound*, February 9, 2016

Websites

Ghostface Killah Chart History, *Billboard*, https://www.billboard.com/music/Ghostface-Killah/chart-history/billboard-200

Nation of Islam, www.noi.org

"Staten Island: A Look Into the Past," TheBrielle.com, https://www.thebrielle.com/staten-island-look-past

https://www.thirteen.org/statenisland/history.html

YouTube

"Action Bronson taking shots at Ghostface Killa?"
www.youtube.com/watch?v=pI2fIbATUPM

"Ghostface Killah Air Out Action Bronson"
www.youtube.com/watch?v=z93IaKPY_Wc

"Ghostface Killah 'Don't Make Me Old School' Interview – Westwood"
www.youtube.com/watch?v=RPaKkZR8DVQ

"Ghostface x Montreality – Interview,"
www.youtube.com/watch?v=hZ6Ha0p9ZUM

"Martin Shkreli -- Shut Your Mouth Ghostface Killah ... My Goons Will Take You Out!!"
www.youtube.com/watch?v=lI9jywQ4cgc&t=27s

"Untitled (Cowboy): Behind Richard Prince's Photographs & Appropriation,"
www.youtube.com/watch?v=bxySP5R-IWs

"Wu Tang Clan with Ed Lover & Doctor Dre in 1993,"
www.youtube.com/watch?v=F8G81d9sFA8

Printed in Great Britain
by Amazon